Exporting to Canada

A Guide for American Companies

T0164273

Self-Counsel Press
(a subsidiary of)
International Self-Counsel Press Ltd.

Self-Counsel Press acknowledges the financial support of the Government of Canada through the Book Publishing Industry Development Program (BPID) for our publishing activities.

Printed in Canada.

First edition: 2001

Cataloguing in Publication Data

Kautz, Gerhard, 1938
    Exporting to Canada: A Guide for American Companies

    (Self-counsel business series)
    ISBN 1-55180-339-9

    1. Export marketing—United States—Handbooks, manuals, etc.
2. Canada—Commerce—Handbooks, manuals, etc. I. Title. II. Series.
HF1416,5,K38 2000   658.8'48'0973   C00-911225-1

Self-Counsel Press Inc.
(a subsidiary of)
International Self-Counsel Press Ltd.

1704 N. State Street	1481 Charlotte Road
Bellingham, WA 98225	North Vancouver, BC V7J 1H1
USA	Canada

Contents

Introduction   ix

1   Why Export to Canada?   1
1. Traditional USA-Canada Trade   1
2. Canadian Economy   3
3. Canadian Dollar   5
4. Shared Language and Culture   6
5. Proximity   7
6. Obtaining International Experience   8
7. Additional Information   8

2   What Is Canada?   9
1. Geography   9
2. Climate   10
3. Population   11

	4.	Government	12
	5.	Canadian Economy	15
	6.	Canadian Government Trade Assistance	15
	7.	Additional Information	16

3 How Does Canada Differ from the USA? — 17
1. Political Structure — 17
2. Elections and Political Parties — 19
3. Law Enforcement — 20
4. Canadian Media — 21
5. Sports and Culture — 21
6. Ethnic Diversity versus Melting Pot — 22

4 The Metric System — 25
1. International System of Units (SI) — 25
2. Basic Concept — 26
3. Length — 28
4. Weight — 28
5. Volume — 28
6. Area — 28
7. Speed — 29
8. Temperature — 29
9. Other Metric Measurements — 29
10. Soft and Hard Conversion — 30

5 North American Free Trade Agreement (NAFTA) — 31
1. Background — 31
2. Harmonized Commodity Description and Coding System (HS) — 33
   2.1 Tariff Reduction Schedules — 33
3. Rules of Origin — 34
4. Business Travel — 36
5. Business Visitors — 38
   5.1 Professionals — 39
   5.2 Intra-Company Transferees — 40
   5.3 Traders and Investors — 41
6. Settling Trade Disputes — 42
7. Additional Information — 42

6	**Consumer Profiles**	45
	1. The Canadian Market	45
	2. Canadian Incomes	47
	3. Expenditure Patterns	48
	4. Multiculturalism	49
	5. Additional Information	50
7	**Labeling, Regulations, and Standards**	51
	1. Food Labeling	52
	2. Non-Food Labeling	54
	3. Textile Labeling	56
	4. Environmental Labeling and Advertising	57
	5. Food Inspection	57
	6. The Competition Act	58
	7. Advertising Regulations	58
	8. Weights and Measures	60
	9. Canadian Standards Association	61
	10. Additional Information	62
8	**Intellectual Property Protection**	65
	1. Intellectual Property in Canada	65
	2. Patents	67
	3. Trademarks	68
	4. Copyright	69
	5. Industrial Design	71
	6. Integrated Circuit Topographies	72
	7. Plant Breeders' Rights	73
	8. Agents	73
	9. Additional Information	73
9	**Transportation and Communication**	75
	1. Road Transportation	76
	2. Air Transportation	76
	3. Rail Transportation	78
	4. Marine Transportation	78
	5. Waterways and Pipelines	79
	6. Telecommunications	80

	7. TV, Radio, and Newspapers	80
	8. Additional Information	81
10	**Government Purchasing**	**83**
	1. Trade Agreements	84
	2. What the Canadian Government Buys	85
	3. Selling to the Canadian Government	86
	4. MERX™: The Electronic Tendering Service	86
	5. Government Source Lists	87
	6. Major Crown Projects	88
	7. Standing Offers	88
	8. Protests	89
	9. Provincial Government Purchases	89
	10. Additional Information	92
11	**Military Purchasing**	**93**
	1. Canada's Military	93
	2. Defense Production Sharing Agreement	95
	3. Military Procurement	96
	4. Major Military Systems Procurement	97
	5. Industrial Participation and Offsets	98
	6. Trade Associations	98
	7. Additional Information	99
12	**Resource Industries**	**101**
	1. Oil, Gas, and Coal	101
	2. Electricity	102
	3. Forestry	103
	4. Fisheries	103
	5. Mining	104
	6. Fur	105
	7. Trade Associations	105
	8. Additional Information	106
13	**Agriculture**	**107**
	1. Farming Regions	107
	2. Field Crops	109
	3. Livestock	109

	4.	Food Processing	110
	5.	Trade Associations	110
	6.	Additional Information	112

14 Manufacturing and Construction Industries — 113

	1.	Overview	114
	2.	Construction	115
	3.	Transportation Equipment	116
	4.	Aerospace Industry	116
	5.	Electrical and Electronic	117
	6.	Chemicals	117
	7.	Clothing	118
	8.	Furniture	119
	9.	Trade Associations	119
	10.	Additional Information	122

15 Service Industries — 123

	1.	Overview	123
	2.	Finance and Real Estate	124
	3.	Health Services	124
	4.	Business Services	125
	5.	Tourism and Hospitality Industries	125
	6.	Trade Associations	126
	7.	Additional Information	129

16 US Government Assistance — 131

	1.	Department of Commerce	131
	2.	Export Assistance Centers	132
	3.	Export Assistance Programs	133
	4.	US Embassy and Consulates in Canada	133
	5.	Canadian Embassy and Consulates in the USA	134
	6.	Additional Information	136

17 Promoting Your Product — 137

	1.	Brochures	137
	2.	Other Marketing Material	138
	3.	Advertising	139
	4.	Trade Shows	139

	5.	Temporary Importing/Exporting of Goods for Exhibiting	140
	6.	Local Briefings and Seminars	141
	7.	Follow-up	141
	8.	Additional Information	142

18 Business Trips to Canada — 143

	1.	Entrance Requirements	143
	2.	Travel Considerations	144
	3.	Currency, Credit Cards, and Banks	145
	4.	Local Business Practices	146
	5.	Goods and Services Tax (GST)	147
	6.	General Considerations	148
	7.	Additional Information	149

19 Shipping into Canada — 151

	1.	Customs Broker	151
	2.	Documentation Required	152
	3.	Duty Payments	156
	4.	Goods and Services Tax	156
	5.	Customs Inspection	157
	6.	Warehousing	157
	7.	Additional Information	158

Appendixes

	A.	NAFTA-Qualifying Professions	159
	B.	Export Assistance Center Locations	165
	C.	Marketing Trip Checklist	177
	D.	Conversion Charts	181

Samples

	1	Certificate of Origin	37
	2	Canada Customs Invoice	153
	3	Form 3B — Canada Customs Coding Form	155

INTRODUCTION

This book is intended to help small- and medium-size American companies successfully export their products to Canada, America's largest trading partner. The book begins with a discussion of why American companies should export to Canada. It then explains the differences between the USA and Canada from a business point of view, including the differences in consumer-related laws. The North American Free Trade Agreement (NAFTA) is discussed, with examples of how American companies can take advantage of it. The various Canadian business sectors are described to enable readers to identify potential business opportunities for their particular product. Sources of assistance, such as the applicable US government offices, are suggested. The book concludes with suggestions on how the reader can —

- ◆ promote his or her product in Canada,
- ◆ make a first business trip to Canada, and

♦ understand the issues associated with shipping products across the international border.

Appendixes provide detailed information on —

♦ NAFTA-qualifying professions for cross-border travel and work,

♦ locations of US government Export Assistance Centers throughout the USA,

♦ a handy checklist for a marketing trip to Canada, and

♦ imperial to metric conversion.

In addition to the information provided, other sources of information are identified throughout the book. These include government publications, government offices, and addresses on the ubiquitous Internet.

The author is the president of GWEM Systems Limited, a Canada-based international marketing consulting company that has done business in more than 40 countries. GWEM also established the Canadian Market Development Services, which assist foreign companies in doing business in Canada. Working with foreign companies, including many American companies, has provided the author with the knowledge and experience to write this book. His book *Exporting*, published by Self-Counsel Press, is in its third printing, and his book *Developing International Markets* was published in 1998 by the Oasis Press of Grants Pass, Oregon.

1
WHY EXPORT TO CANADA?

Canada is the biggest trading partner of the United States. The two countries share the same language, culture, and the world's largest undefended border. The Canadian economy is growing rapidly and is hungry for imports. These facts, plus the chance to easily gain international business experience, are why you should look north for new markets.

1. Traditional USA-Canada Trade

When the average American is asked who is their country's largest trading partner, they usually guess Japan, China, or a European country. Few realize that the answer is Canada. In fact, the USA exports more to Canada than it does to the next two trading partners combined. The table below shows the value of US exports to the top ten countries in the last five years.

US Exports to Top Ten Countries
(In billions of dollars)

Country	1993	1994	1995	1996	1997 (estimated)
Canada	92.4	104.3	113.3	119.3	134.6
Mexico	40.2	49.1	44.9	54.7	68.5
Japan	45.9	51.5	61.0	64.0	61.6
United Kingdom	24.6	24.8	26.3	28.7	33.1
South Korea	14.4	17.5	24.5	25.5	26.8
Germany	17.9	18.2	21.2	22.2	23.4
Taiwan	15.5	16.3	18.0	16.9	18.3
Netherlands	12.2	13.0	16.0	15.5	18.3
Singapore	10.7	11.7	13.6	14.7	15.6
France	12.5	12.7	13.3	13.6	15.1

The table shows that, on average, the USA exports more than $10 billion to Canada every month. Wouldn't you like just a tiny fraction of that business? Your answer probably is, "Yes, but do they buy my type of products?" The following table may answer that question for you. It shows the major categories of American exports to Canada. However, whether your product is on the list or not, you should still consider the Canadian market. After all, if Americans are buying your wares, Canadians should as well.

Major Categories of American Exports to Canada

Category	1996 Value (Billions of Dollars)
Motor Vehicle Parts and Accessories	15.962
Motor Vehicles and Car Bodies	12.072
Electronic Components	3.986
Semiconductors and Related Devices	2.991
Plastics Materials and Resins	2.508

Category	1996 Value (Billions of Dollars)
Internal Combustion Engines	2.378
Blast Furnaces and Steel Mills	1.741
Construction Machinery	1.437
Industrial Organic Chemicals	1.422
Refrigeration and Heating Equipment	1.411
Paper Mills	1.299
Telephone Apparatus	1.291
Furniture and Fixtures	1.289
Plastics Products	1.139
Engine Electrical Equipment	1.137
Farm Machinery and Equipment	1.128
Industrial Inorganic Chemicals	1.043
Process Control Instruments	1.043
Aircraft Engines and Engine Parts	0.999
Valves and Pipe Fittings	0.977
Aircraft Parts and Equipment	0.925
Household Audio and Video Equipment	0.903
Current-Carrying Wiring Devices	0.865
Aluminum Sheet, Plate, and Foil	0.860
Petroleum Refining	0.829

2. Canadian Economy

Canada is a trading nation, with about 33 percent of its economy depending on export. However, like most trade dependent countries, it also is a huge importer. In 1996 imports made up 29 percent of the Canadian Gross Domestic Product (GDP). More than half of these imports are associated with the manufacturing industries in the country. These are in two categories. The first is the materials industries must import to use in the products they manufacture (e.g., microprocessor chips and other electronic components for Canada's thriving telecommunications industry). Much of this comes from the USA. The second category is the machinery required to do the manufacturing. If your product fits into either of these two manufacturing categories, you could be targeting billions of dollars worth of business in Canada. If your product is not used in a manufacturing process, you have an equally large, new market.

Canada's heavy economic dependence on manufacturing is a major difference between Canada and the USA. The following table shows that the US is proportionally more dependent on the service industries than is Canada, and Canada is more involved in goods producing than is the USA:

USA and Canada Economic Divisions as Percentage of GDP

Country	Goods Producing	Services	Government
USA	21 percent	66 percent	13 percent
Canada	34 percent	49 percent	17 percent

The compounded average annual growth rate of the manufacturing sector of the Canadian economy, over the period 1990 to 1995, was 2 percent. The following table shows the areas of the manufacturing sector, the related contribution to the Canadian GDP, and the compounded average annual growth rate:

Canadian Manufacturing Industries Growth (1990–95)

Industry	GDP (1995) ($ Billions)	Annual Growth (1990 to 1995)
Transportation	15.8	3.7
Electric/Electronic	12.7	9.6
Food	10.2	1.5
Chemical	8.2	1.1
Paper	7.9	0.9
Primary Metal	7.6	3.5
Fabricated Metal	6.3	-0.5
Wood	5.1	0.9
Printing/Publishing	4.3	-5.6

Industry	GDP (1995) ($ Billions)	Annual Growth (1990 to 1995)
Machinery	3.8	1.0
Other Manufacturing	2.6	2.0
Non-metallic Mineral	2.6	-2.9
Beverage	2.5	1.1
Clothing	2.2	-2.1
Plastic	2.2	3.2
Petroleum	2.1	0.4
Furniture/Fixture	1.8	1.0
Rubber	1.6	7.5
Primary Textile	1.0	1.2
Textile Products	0.9	-1.9
Tobacco	0.5	-0.9
Leather	0.2	-4.0

The growth rates discussed above are impressive, but the Paris-based Organization for Economic Co-operation and Development (OECD) is predicting much higher growth rates for the Canadian economy in the next few years. With this growth will come an even higher demand for imported products. You may be able to satisfy some of that demand.

Note: Much of the previous information is provided by the Canadian government's Department of Industry, referred to as Industry Canada, on their Web site: <www.ic.gc.ca>.

3. Canadian Dollar

Many exporters looking to Canada think that the low Canadian dollar would make their products too expensive for the Canadians to buy. The Canadian dollar floats on the open market, and, as such, fluctuates with the world currency trading market. In recent years it has ranged between about 0.64 to 0.85 US dollars per Canadian dollar. The low international value of the dollar has made Canadian exports very competitively priced on the world market, and has helped to boost Canadian exports.

But what about imports to Canada? One would think that as the dollar drops, Canadians would be less able to afford to purchase goods from outside the country, and the number of imports would drop as well. If this was the case, it would not be good for foreign exporters. However, this is not the case according to *Export News*, published by the Alliance of Manufacturers & Exporters Canada. Over the last 15 years, as the Canadian dollar fell, Canadian exports increased, and surprisingly, so did imports into Canada. The explanation for this lies in the fact that in order for Canadian companies to expand their exports, they have to import more materials and equipment to produce the exports. Also, with more exports, the Canadian standard of living rises and the people can afford more imports.

Do not let the low Canadian dollar scare you. It may affect some imports into the country, but on the whole it actually increases imports. You will also be pleasantly surprised during your business trips to Canada when you are able to stay in luxury hotels and eat in fine restaurants for considerably less American money than you would have to pay back in the USA.

4. Shared Language and Culture

Canada and the USA have very much in common, and this makes it considerably easier to do business between the two countries than with other countries. There are some small differences in the English language, mainly in the spelling. Canadians favor — sorry, favour — the British way of spelling. For example, they tend to use 'our' rather than just 'or' in words like labor, favor, and neighbor. They also pronounce some words differently from Americans, but generally the language is the same. It is quite possible that Americans from the northern states will understand Canadians better than they do their fellow citizens from some of the southern states.

The only language problem you will encounter is the requirement for French in some instances. French is legally mandatory only in the province of Quebec, but most businesspeople speak English. Consumer products sold in Canada require both English and French labeling (which will be discussed in a later chapter), but this is not a big problem. You might want to be aware of the ongoing question of Quebec separation, but don't worry about it, and don't discuss it.

Canadians are fiercely proud of their culture, but in fact it differs only slightly from that of the USA. Canadians enjoy all of the popular US movies and TV programs. Many big-name entertainers in the USA are Canadian — there is even a popular US national TV news announcer who is Canadian as well. In sports there is no border between the two countries. The National Hockey League teams in the USA may be dominated by Canadians, but the pro baseball and basketball teams in Toronto, Montreal, and Vancouver consist mainly of American players. (Don't forget that the Toronto Blue Jays won the baseball World Series two years in a row!) There is considerable cross-pollination of culture between the two countries.

Business practices in both countries are pretty much the same. If anything, Canadians are less aggressive than Americans. But don't let that fool you. Remember the billions of dollars worth of exports the USA sells to Canada each year. Well, Canada sells much more back to the US. Nevertheless, you will find it a lot easier to do business in Canada than in many other countries.

5. Proximity

Another good reason for you to consider exporting to Canada is its proximity. Don't let the map scare you. Although Canada is physically larger than the USA, the majority of the Canadian population lives within a hundred miles of the US border. You may find that Canadian business opportunities are closer to you than those in the USA. For example, if your business is located on the Eastern Seaboard, you are much closer to the main Canadian market than you are to California.

Transportation links abound between the two countries. There are direct air links between the major Canadian and US cities. American trains run into Canadian terminals well within the country. Major freeways of each country meet at the border, and the crossing is usually a matter of only a brief Customs stop. The large numbers of transport trucks crossing in both directions at these highway border crossings also illustrate the huge volume of trade between the two countries.

6. Obtaining International Experience

Probably the best reason to start your export activities with Canada is to give yourself some basic experience in international business. While there are many similarities between Canada and the USA, Canada is, of course, a different country. As a business person, you will have to deal with different laws, packaging, metrics, and other issues, including the international border. This book is intended to help you address these issues before you have to confront them. But because the problems you will encounter will not be nearly as difficult as those you would face in other countries, you can think of Canada as your training-wheel phase of exporting.

7. Additional Information

1. Industry Canada home page on the Internet at <www.ic.gc.ca>.

2. *Basic Guide to Exporting*, US Department of Commerce, available on the Internet at <www.doc.gov> (home page); <http://mena-peacenet.nist.gov/US/ Ex-guide/intro.html>.

3. *ABCs of Exporting to Canada*, US Department of Commerce, available on the Internet at <www.mac.doc.gov/nafta/7401.htm>.

4. Business Fact Sheet: Canada, US Department of Commerce, available on the Internet at <www.mac.doc.gov/nafta/7101.htm>.

2
WHAT IS CANADA?

Canada is a large, sparsely populated country. It is similar to the USA in many ways, yet there are distinct differences. This chapter provides an overall description of Canada, and chapter 3 discusses how it differs from the USA.

1. Geography

Canada is the world's second largest country, although much of it is uninhabitable. It stretches mainly from the 49th parallel that is its common border with the USA, north to the high arctic, and from the Atlantic to the Pacific Oceans. (There is a small area around the Great Lakes that dips below the 49th parallel and is in fact at about the same latitude as northern California.) The area of Canada is about ten million square kilometers, and there are six time zones within the country.

The geography is as diverse as that of the USA. The east coast, or Atlantic Canada (the provinces of Newfoundland, Nova Scotia, New Brunswick, and Prince Edward Island), is mostly rugged terrain that is unsuitable for farming. Southern Quebec and Ontario have rolling hills and arable land used for dairy farming and industry, while in the northern part of these two provinces the land is a harsh mixture of rocky forest and lakes. The central prairies (Manitoba, Saskatchewan and Alberta) are flat, with grain fields stretching as far as the eye can see. Western Alberta shares the stunning beauty of the Rocky Mountains with British Columbia, and BC also has the spectacular Pacific coast. The northern part of Canada, from about the 60th parallel north, is covered with snow and ice for most of the year.

2. Climate

The Canadian climate is as diverse as the geography. The east coast can have heavy snowfalls in winter, with considerable fog and rain the rest of the year. Ontario and Quebec can have bitterly cold winter days and heavy snowfalls, but the summers can be hot and humid. The prairies also experience very cold winter temperatures and heavy snowfalls, but the summers are warm and pleasant. The west coast weather is influenced by the Pacific Ocean, with moderate temperatures seldom dropping below freezing in the winters and remaining mild in the summers. In the North the summers last only about two months. The following table shows the average temperature and precipitation in some Canadian cities:

Average Temperature and Precipitation in Canadian Cities

City	Month	Temperature (°F)		Rain (inches)	Snow (inches)
		Maximum	Minimum		
Vancouver	Jan	42	32	5.18	0.81
	Apr	55	41	2.95	0.20
	Jul	71	54	1.42	0.00
	Oct	56	44	4.54	0.00
Winnipeg	Jan	12	-8	0.20	7.56
	Apr	51	28	0.52	3.46

City	Month	Temperature (°F) Maximum	Minimum	Rain (inches)	Snow (inches)
Winnipeg	Jul	79	53	2.32	0.00
	Oct	53	29	0.54	2.99
Toronto	Jan	28	12	0.73	12.72
	Apr	53	33	2.20	2.87
	Jul	80	58	3.02	0.00
	Oct	57	38	2.44	0.43
Montreal	Jan	22	5	0.82	18.78
	Apr	51	33	2.46	4.29
	Jul	79	60	3.37	0.00
	Oct	55	38	2.87	1.02
Halifax	Jan	31	16	3.21	19.25
	Apr	46	32	3.72	5.55
	Jul	71	56	3.85	0.00
	Oct	56	41	4.72	0.71

3. Population

The 1996 census found the population of Canada to be 28.8 million, about one-tenth that of the USA. The majority of this population lives within 100 miles of the US border. About 77 percent live in cities or towns, leaving only about 23 percent in rural areas. The table below shows the population of some of the major cities:

Population of Major Canadian Cities

City	Population
Toronto	4.26 million
Montreal	3.33 million
Vancouver	1.81 million
Ottawa (region)	1.01 million
Edmonton	0.86 million

City	Population
Calgary	0.74 million
Winnipeg	0.65 million
Halifax	0.32 million

Canada continues to welcome immigrants at the rate of about 200,000 per year, resulting in a very wide mix of ethnic origins from Asia, Europe, the Middle East, and the Caribbean. Both English and French are the official languages of Canada, with about a quarter of the population speaking French, mainly in Quebec, New Brunswick, and eastern Ontario. However, other languages are also freely spoken throughout the country. For example, the third most popular language spoken in Ottawa, the nation's capital, is Arabic, while Ukrainian is popular in Edmonton.

The predominant religion is Christianity, with 47.3 percent of the population Roman Catholic and 41.2 percent Protestant. Eastern Orthodox is 1.5 percent of the population, and Jewish is 1.2 percent. Other religions include Islam, Hinduism, Sikhism, and Buddhism. About 7.4 percent of the population have no religious preference.

Canada requires that children attend school until the age of 15 or 16, depending on the province. This has resulted in about half of the population being high school graduates. Over half of these high school graduates continue on to postsecondary educational institutions, resulting in more than 25 percent of the work force having a university or college degree.

Canadians enjoy a high standard of living and quality of life. They have the second highest incomes in the world, after Americans. Over 65 percent of Canadians own their own homes. In 1999 the United Nations declared Canada to be the best country in the world in which to live.

4. Government

Canada is a constitutional monarchy. It is part of the British Commonwealth, and technically the Canadian head of state is the Queen of England. However, since 1867 Canada has been a self-governing dominion, and in 1931 was granted full independence from Britain. In practice the Queen is merely a figurehead who does not exercise any authority over the Canadian people.

The legislative power is the Parliament of Canada. It consists of a 301-member elected House of Commons, and a 112-member Senate. The leader of the party with the most elected members in the House of Commons is the prime minister, the leader of Canada. The responsibilities of this federal government are shown in the following table:

Responsibilities of the Federal Government

National Defense (Canadians spell it *defence*)

International Trade and Commerce

Criminal Law (including the RCMP[1])

Monetary System

Immigration

Fisheries

Shipping

Railways

Aeronautics

Telecommunications

Atomic Energy

Note: 1. The Royal Canadian Mounted Police is the federal police force, somewhat similar to the FBI in the USA. However, some provinces and municipalities also hire the RCMP to be their own police forces.

There are ten provinces and three territories, shown in the following table:

Canadian Provinces and Territories

Province/Territory	Population	Capital City
Alberta	2,545,600	Edmonton
British Columbia	3,282,100	Victoria

Province/Territory	Population	Capital City
Manitoba	1,091,900	Winnipeg
New Brunswick	723,900	Fredericton
Newfoundland	568,500	St. John's
Nova Scotia	899,900	Halifax
Ontario	10,084,900	Toronto
Prince Edward Island	129,800	Charlottetown
Quebec	6,895,900	Quebec City
Saskatchewan	988,900	Regina
Northwest Territories[1]	39,672	Yellowknife
Nunavut Territory	24,900	Iqaluit
Yukon Territory	27,800	Whitehorse

Note: 1. In 1999, the former Northwest Territories were divided into two territories. The new one is called Nunavut, and, at the time of writing, the remaining area has retained the name Northwest Territories.

Each province and territory has its own elected parliament. The leader of the political party with the most elected members in the parliament is the premier of the province. (In Quebec this person is called the prime minister.) The table below shows the areas of responsibility of the provinces:

Provincial Areas of Responsibility

Natural Resources

Education

Property and Civil Rights

Health System

Social Security

Municipal Institutions

Municipal governments within the provinces, such as city governments, are responsible for their local matters including police, fire-fighting, etcetera.

5. Canadian Economy

Canada has one of the strongest economies in the world. It is second only to the USA in terms of per capita purchasing power. It is the eighth largest trading nation in the world, and is also very active in investment throughout the world. The Gross Domestic Product (GDP) in 1996 was over $500 billion, and the GDP per capita was $22,300. The inflation rate in 1997 was around 1.2 percent and it remains steady between 1.0 percent and 2.0 percent.

Canada is a trading nation and most of its trade is with the USA. In 1996 Canada exported about $193 billion worth of goods and services, and imported about $163 billion. This left a very favorable trade surplus of about $24 billion.

It is interesting to note that the province of Ontario by itself is the second largest trading partner of the USA, with total trade of about $100 billion. Ontario exports more automobiles to the USA than does all the rest of the world.

Other aspects of the Canadian economy are discussed throughout this book, mainly those that affect your export decision.

6. Canadian Government Trade Assistance

The Canadian government Department of Industry, or Industry Canada, is responsible for trade and commerce in the country. (The Department of Foreign Affairs and International Trade also has a role, but mainly with regard to exports from Canada.) This institution can provide you with considerable information about Canadian business. Much of the information in this book comes from Industry Canada. You can access Industry Canada through the Canadian embassy in Washington, or through the many Canadian consulates throughout the USA. However, the easiest initial contact may be through their STRATEGIS Internet site at <http://strategis.ic.gc.ca/>. This will answer many of your questions, and hot link you to other relevant sources of information.

7. Additional Information

1. Canadian government Web site: http://canada.gc.ca

2. Web site for Industry Canada: www.ic.gc.ca

3
HOW DOES CANADA DIFFER FROM THE USA?

On the surface, Canada and Canadians may appear very similar to the USA and Americans, and in most ways this is true. However, there are a number of differences that you should be aware of, as some of them may affect your business. The business-related differences between the two countries are discussed in this chapter.

1. Political Structure

Canada has a federal government and a government for each of the provinces and territories. The provinces are very similar to the states of the USA, yet the political systems of the federal and provincial governments are quite different from the American system. You should be aware of these differences if you are doing business with any level of Canadian government.

As mentioned in the previous chapter, the Canadian government is a constitutional monarchy. That is, the Queen of England is technically the head of state, rather than an elected president. In practice, though, Canada does have an elected head of state. The Prime Minister, who is the leader of the political party with the most elected members in the House of Commons, leads the country. The Queen, in fact, plays a very small role in the governing of Canada, and there is an increasing debate within the country about her future there.

The other major difference between the American and Canadian political structures is that Canada has a parliamentary system rather than a congressional system like the USA. As in many other countries, the parliament is patterned after the British parliamentary system. It consists of two houses: the House of Commons and the Senate. The House of Commons is the highest elected body in the country. The members are elected in each of the 295 ridings (similar to US Congressional Districts) across the country. The House of Commons is somewhat similar to the US House of Representatives, with one major difference. The political party with the most members is the ruling party in Canada, and includes the prime minister and the cabinet.

The Senate has 112 members, but unlike the USA, they are not elected. They are appointed for life, or to age 75, by the ruling party at the time when a seat becomes vacant. Traditionally, the Senate seats must have equal representation from all of the provinces and territories. There is considerable debate going on in Canada as to the future of the Senate, with many Canadians wanting it to become an elected body.

The cabinet consists of members of the House of Commons who have been appointed to the cabinet by the prime minister. This is another big difference between Canada and the USA. The cabinet ministers themselves are elected by the people, although at the time of the election the voters do not know who will be cabinet ministers. The voters know only who the leader of each party is — who will become prime minister if his or her party gets the most seats in the House of Commons. The prime minister then chooses the cabinet ministers from the members of the party who were elected. Each cabinet minister heads up a department of the government, such as the Department of National Defence or the Department of Industry. Since the ministers of each department usually change at each election, and sometimes between elections, continuity is maintained by senior civil servants called deputy ministers. These people come from the ranks of the permanent civil service.

The governments of the provinces and territories are very similar in structure to the federal system. The premier, or head of the province, is the leader of the political party with the most elected members in the provincial legislature, which is the equivalent of the federal House of Commons. Provincial cabinet ministers come from the elected members of the provincial ruling party.

2. Elections and Political Parties

With the exception of municipal elections, which are held on a regular basis about every two years, elections in Canada can happen at any time. This is an important point to remember if you are doing business with the federal or provincial governments. There is usually a hiatus of government purchasing or spending on large programs leading up to an election and for a while thereafter.

According to the Canadian constitution, federal elections must be held at least every five years. It is up to the government in power to call the election, and it can be at any time. Some elections have even been called within months of a previous election. Typically, the government, or ruling party, tries to have the election at the time that would most favor it (e.g., if the economy is strong, unemployment is down, and the polls say that the people are relatively happy with the way they are being governed). Usually, elections are held about every four years. Spring and fall are the preferred times of the year for an election, in order to avoid the Canadian winter and to let the people enjoy the summer.

There is no limitation on the number of political parties allowed in Canada, or what they represent. Even the Communist party is allowed to run in Canadian elections. They don't get many votes, but they still manage to field the odd candidate at election time. The main political parties run the political spectrum from left (New Democrat Party, or NDP), to center left (Liberal Party), to center right (Progressive Conservative or PC Party), to right (Canadian Alliance, previously the Reform party). Most election campaigns are based on the party's platform and the leader, who will become the prime minister if his or her party can elect the most members. The party with the second most elected members becomes the official opposition, and its leader is the leader of the opposition. A party must have a certain minimum number of elected members to be recognized as an official party.

3. Law Enforcement

For those readers interested in marketing to the police forces of Canada, there are some similarities to and some differences from US police forces. The table below gives some guidelines on the similarities and differences based on US law enforcement agencies:

Canadian Law Enforcement Agencies	
US **Agency**	**Canadian Equivalent**
FBI	Canada's national police force is the Royal Canadian Mounted Police (RCMP), whose name and tradition dates back to the mid 1800s. The RCMP is also contracted by many of the provinces and smaller municipalities to be their police force.
CIA	The Canadian Security Intelligence Service (CSIS) is responsible for monitoring subversive activities within the country. They have no mandate outside of Canada.
State Police	Ontario has the Ontario Provincial Police (OPP), and Quebec has the Quebec Provincial Police (QPP), or *Sûreté du Québec* as it is called in French. All other provinces and territories contract with the RCMP.
City Police	Each large city has its own police force. The smaller ones contract with the RCMP, the OPP, or the QPP.
Municipal Police	Some smaller jurisdictions have their own police force, but most contract with the RCMP, the OPP, or the QPP.
Highway Patrol	RCMP, OPP, QPP, city or municipal police forces, depending on the jurisdiction.

The security business is a growing industry in Canada, as it is in most parts of the world. However, there is one major difference between Canada and the US. Almost all Canadian civilian security personnel are unarmed. You should also note that small arms are strictly controlled in Canada.

4. Canadian Media

The print media in Canada is somewhat similar to that in the USA. Newspapers are very locally aimed, although some, like the *National Post* and the *Globe and Mail*, offer a daily national edition. The major newspapers are owned by a few large corporations. There are many Canadian magazines, but most of the popular US magazines are readily available throughout Canada. Some of these produce a Canadian edition with a portion of Canadian content in addition to the regular US content. There are certain advertising rules associated with these US-owned magazines sold in Canada, which you may want to look into before you advertise in them.

The broadcast media, TV and radio, is overseen by the Canadian Radio-Television and Telecommunications Commission (CRTC). The CRTC grants broadcasting licenses and has the power to withdraw them if certain criteria are not met, such as a defined amount of Canadian content. However, most of the popular US TV and radio programs are also available on the Canadian stations, or Canadians simply tune in to American broadcasts from US cities near the border. There are three major TV networks in Canada: the Canadian Television network (CTV), the Global Television network, and the Canadian Broadcasting Corporation (CBC).

The CBC is a distinctly Canadian enterprise. It is a government-owned radio and television company with several networks: the English-language CBC TV; the French-language CBC TV; Radio One, which carries news and information programming; Radio Two, which concentrates on classical music and the arts; and the French radio equivalents. The CBC radio networks carry no advertising and are fully funded by the government. The CBC TV networks do carry advertising, and operate like most other TV networks, but offer more Canadian content. There are also some publicly funded TV stations, but these are usually subsidized by the federal or provincial governments.

5. Sports and Culture

Canadians enjoy the same sports as Americans, but with different emphasis. Everyone knows that Canada is a land of ice hockey (although lacrosse is the offical national sport). Kids start playing in organized hockey leagues before they go to school. Other winter sports such as curling and skiing are also very popular. Summer sports such as baseball and golf are played with equal vigor during the summer season. Football is not as popular in high schools and universities as it is in the US, although it is still played. Canadians are also increasingly interested in soccer.

Professional sports are very similar to those in the US, and in fact most of the major pro-sports leagues transcend the border. The National Hockey League has had Canadian and American teams for over half a century. The Vancouver Grizzlies and the Toronto Raptors are part of the National Basketball Association. (The inventor of basketball was a Canadian.) The Montreal Expos of the National Baseball League and the Toronto Blue Jays of the American Baseball League are also well known. (Canadians are quick to remind Americans that for two years in a row the Blue Jays won the World Series, making it a truly international event.) The only major American professional sport that does not have a Canadian team is football. This is because there is a Canadian Football League (CFL) that plays a slightly different version of the game. Nevertheless, most of the players in the CFL are American.

Canadians are very proud of their culture, but have difficulty defining it. They insist that it is different from US culture, and in some ways it is, yet in most ways it is quite similar. This book will not enter into the debate, and suggests that you don't try to argue the point with a Canadian.

6. Ethnic Diversity versus Melting Pot

Both Canada and the USA are largely made up of immigrants from all over the world. From the beginning, however, there has been a difference in how new immigrants are assimilated into each country. The American approach is that of a 'melting pot,' in which newcomers are encouraged to blend into the rest of the population. In Canada, ethnic differences are respected and encouraged. There is even a federal government Department of Multiculturalism that fosters, promotes, and funds ethnic activities and events.

Mother-tongue usage, in addition to English and French, is tolerated and encouraged. In some cities the emergency 911 telephone number has interpreters available for several languages. Instructions on how to fill out common government application forms, such as those for automobile licenses, are sometimes posted in languages other than the two official ones. There is also a growing number of radio and TV programs in various languages.

Ethnic festivals are popular events throughout Canada, enjoyed by all. Chinese New Year celebrations are popular in Vancouver and Toronto. Toronto also offers the annual Caribana parade, which honors a large ethnic community with Caribbean origins. There are social clubs organized along ethnic lines in every Canadian city. If your product can appeal to a certain ethnic group or groups, you will find a well-defined market for it in Canada.

4
THE METRIC SYSTEM

The United States is the only country that does not use the metric system in its measurements. Canada, along with the rest of the non-US world, uses the International System of Units, commonly referred to as the metric system. In order to do business in Canada you have to know and in most cases use the metric system. You will have to do this if you plan to export to the rest of world as well. The chart in Appendix D provides some conversion factors for some of the measurements commonly used in the USA.

1. International System of Units (SI)

In 1875 seventeen nations met and signed the Treaty of the Metre, which set up an international body to standardize measurements throughout the world. Many other countries have since signed the treaty. Canada signed it in 1907. The treaty set up regular conferences called *la Conference Generale des Poids et Mesures* or CGPM. In 1960 the CGPM adopted the International System of Units, which uses the abbreviation SI. In 1971 Canada passed the Weights and Measures Act that adopted the SI.

The SI uses seven basic units of measurement:

♦ meter for length;

♦ kilogram for mass (weight);

♦ Kelvin for thermodynamic temperature;

♦ second for time;

♦ ampere for electric current;

♦ mole for amount of substance;

♦ candela for luminous intensity.

This book will address only the main units associated with international trade; that is, the measurements of length, mass, temperature, and the derived units for volume and speed.

In order to carry out international trade, you will probably have to use the SI units of measurement. But there are many other advantages to using the system, such as the following:

♦ There are only a few easily defined units.

♦ All multiples and sub-multiples are in powers of ten.

♦ There is a direct relationship between the units of length, volume, and weight.

2. Basic Concept

The metric concept is very simple in that there are only a few basic units, and the relationships between various sizes of the basic units are multiples or sub-multiples of ten. The basic units and their symbols are shown in the following table:

Basic SI Units		
Measurement	Unit	Symbol
Length	meter	m
Weight	gram	g

Measurement	Unit	Symbol
Volume	liter	L and l
Temperature	degree Celsius	°C
Time	second	s

Multiples and sub-multiples of these units are expressed by adding prefixes to the unit names, such as the prefix "kilo" attached to "meter" to denote a thousand meters as a "kilometer." The following table provides some of the more common prefixes:

Common Metric Prefixes

Prefix	Symbol	Multiplies Basic Unit By
mega	M	1,000,000
kilo	k	1,000
hecto	h	100
deca	da	10
deci	d	0.1
centi	c	0.01
milli	m	0.001
micro	μ	0.000001

These symbols of the SI units are used consistently throughout the world, so they are applicable in any language. Some of the rules to use in writing the symbols are as follows:

- Symbols are written in lower case (m, g, s), except when the unit name comes from a proper name (L, C).
- There is no spacing between the prefix symbol and the unit symbol (km, kg).
- Symbols are never pluralized.
- Periods are not used after symbols.
- A space is inserted between a number and a symbol (17 m).

3. Length

The basic unit of length is the meter. The actual definition of a meter is the length equal to 1,650,763.73 wavelengths in vacuum of the radiation corresponding to the transition between the levels 2p10 and 5d2 of the krypton-86 atom. However, you can think of it as about one yard or 39 inches. You can also think of a kilometer as being about 2/3 of a mile, although the actual conversion is one kilometer equals 0.62 miles. Conversely, one mile equals 1.6093 kilometers.

4. Weight

The basic unit of mass or weight is the gram. The actual definition of a gram is based on the international kilogram that is a cylinder of platinum-iridium alloy kept by the International Bureau of Weights and Measures in Paris. You can, however, think of a kilogram as being a little more than two pounds, or one pound equals about half a kilogram. The actual conversion is one pound equals 0.45359 kilograms, or one kilogram equals 2.2046 pounds.

The metric ton, referred to as tonne (t), is the weight of one cubic meter of water. However, you can consider it to be about equivalent to the imperial ton. The actual conversion is one ton equals 0.90718 tonnes, or one tonne equals 1.1023 tons.

5. Volume

The most common unit of volume or capacity is the liter. In actual fact it is a cubic decimeter; that is, 1/100 of a cubic meter. You can think of a liter as being just a bit more than a liquid US quart. The actual conversion is one liquid US quart equals 0.9463 liters, or one liter equals 1.0567 quarts.

6. Area

The most common unit of area you will run across is square meters, but you may also have to deal with property sizes, which are usually expressed in hectares (ha). A hectare is an area 100 meters by 100 meters, or 10,000 square meters. It is equivalent to 2.471 acres. You can think of a hectare as being about two and a half acres.

7. Speed

The main metric speed measurement you will have to contend with in Canada is the driving speed limit, which is in kilometers per hour. The usual highway speed limit is 100 kilometers per hour (km/hr), and the common road speed limit is 50 km/hr. A good rule of thumb is that 100 km/hr is 60 miles per hour, and that 50 km/hr is 30 miles per hour. In actual fact these are 62.14 and 31.07 respectively. When you rent a car in Canada you will notice that the speedometer is in kilometers per hour, although miles per hour is usually also shown in smaller print.

8. Temperature

The temperature measurement that is used in the SI is based on the Kelvin scale that starts at absolute zero (about -460°F). This is not very convenient, so the Celsius scale was developed. It uses the same individual degree size as the Kelvin scale, but is based on zero degrees Celsius (0°C) as the freezing point of water, and 100°C as the boiling point of water. Temperatures below zero degrees Celsius are referred to as minus. For example, zero degrees Fahrenheit is about minus eighteen degrees Celsius (-18°C).

A simple way to get an approximate idea of what Celsius temperatures are in Fahrenheit is to double the Celsius value and then add 30. For example, for 20 degrees Celsius: double 20 to get 40, then add 30 to get 70, the approximate Fahrenheit value. The actual value is 68 degrees Fahrenheit, but this quick calculation method is usually close enough. The exact conversion formulas are shown in Appendix D.

9. Other Metric Measurements

You will be happy to know that most other metric measurements that you will run across are the same as the ones you currently use. The basic unit of time is the second, and the minutes, hours, and days are what you normally use. Some people refer to the twenty-four hour clock as 'metric time' or 'military time.' In this system you add 12 to the p.m. hours, and express everything in hundreds. For example, 3 p.m. is 1500 (3 + 12 x 100), and 8:15 a.m. is 0815. In Canada both systems are used, but the standard a.m. and p.m. designations are far more common.

The metric unit for electric current is the ampere, which is the same as in the USA. Similarly, volts, watts, and kilowatts are the same in Canada as in the USA. You will also be happy to know that the household electrical system in Canada is similar to that of the US; that is, 120 volts and 60 cycles. (In much of the rest of the world it is different. For example, in Europe the standard household electrical supply is 220 volts, 50 cycle.)

10. Soft and Hard Conversion

When Canada went through the process of converting to metric back in the 1970s, they used the terms soft conversion and hard conversion. These two conversion approaches may also be applicable to your business in dealing with Canada or any other non-US country.

Soft conversion is the easiest to do. You simply change the measurement system by converting your current measurement into the metric equivalent. For example, a pint of olive oil becomes 0.473 liters, or 473 milliliters of olive oil. A yard of cloth becomes 0.9144 meters or 91.4 centimeters.

Hard conversion is much more difficult. Here you actually change your container or measurement to the nearest rounded-off metric equivalent. Using the above example, you would have to change the container of your olive oil so that it is 0.5 liters, or 500 milliliters. In order to do business in Canada, and the rest of the world, you may have to do this hard conversion. Please refer to the labeling requirements described in chapter 7.

5
NORTH AMERICAN FREE TRADE AGREEMENT (NAFTA)

NAFTA is a major trade agreement between the USA, Canada, and Mexico. It reduces trade barriers between the countries, and increases business opportunities. There are a number of issues about NAFTA that you should know. This chapter covers most of these issues in a broad way, with references to other sources of information for further detail.

1. Background

There is a long history of trade agreements between the USA and Canada, most notably in the period since the Second World War, beginning with the Principles of Economic Cooperation in 1950. The Defense Production Sharing Agreement of 1959 basically removed the border between the two countries with regard to the development and production of military equipment. The most significant of these bilateral trade agreements was the Autopact of 1965, which eliminated tariffs on vehicles and original equipment parts, and in effect integrated the industry of the two countries. In 1985 these arrangements were reaffirmed in Quebec City by President Reagan and Prime Minister Mulroney.

On January 1, 1989, the United States-Canada Free Trade Agreement (FTA) came into being. This agreement eliminated all tariffs between the USA and Canada on Canadian and US goods. It also reduced or eliminated a number of other trade barriers between the two countries.

The North American Free Trade Agreement (NAFTA) between the USA, Canada, and Mexico contains many of the provisions of the FTA. It came into effect on January 1, 1994, and in so doing created the world's largest free trade zone. It is still being phased in, but most of the provisions of the agreement are currently in effect. NAFTA is a very complex agreement, and all the issues cannot be covered in this book. Additional information pertaining to your product can be obtained from the information sources listed at the end of this chapter. The major benefit of NAFTA is the elimination of tariffs between the countries, but there are also many other benefits such as:

♦ Allowance of cross-border trade in services such as professional services;

♦ Liberalization of transportation services; and

♦ Better access for professionals such as engineers. (See Appendix A for a list of NAFTA-qualifying professions.)

There are two key aspects of NAFTA that determine the status of your products with regard to the tariff reduction schedule. The first is the Harmonized Commodity Description and Coding System, and the second is the Rules of Origin. Both of these are discussed in the next sections.

2. Harmonized Commodity Description and Coding System (HS)

The Harmonized Commodity Description and Coding System (HS) is used by the Customs Services of the USA, Canada, and Mexico. It has several purposes, but the main one is to identify the tariffs that apply to goods in trade. The HS, or Harmonized System, is also used for freight documentation and reporting trade statistics between the countries. You can find out more about the HS number for your product by contacting the Census Bureau Foreign Trade Division at (301) 457-3047.

The HS is very logically structured. Products are arranged into 97 chapters based on economic activity. Each chapter is divided into headings, subheadings, and tariff items. The chapter, heading, and subheading numbers are the same for all the countries using the HS system, and only the last two digits, the tariff items, are assigned by the importing country. For example, all tomato sauces are classified in the HS subheading 2103.20, regardless of the country of import. However, tomato ketchup is specifically classified by tariff item 2103.20.10 in Canada, 2103.20.40 in the USA, and 2103.20.01 in Mexico.

The following example, taken from the Revenue Canada publication *NAFTA Rules of Origin*, illustrates this HS coding system:

Harmonized System (HS) Example of Item 9504.20.21

Chapter 95.........................Toys, games, and sports requisites

Heading 95.04.......................Table or parlor games

Subheading 9504.20................Articles for billiards and accessories

Tariff item 9504.20.21...............Billiard tables

In order to export to Canada (or Mexico) under the rules of NAFTA, you have to establish the HS number of your product. All associated paperwork will be based on that number.

2.1 Tariff Reduction Schedules

Prior to the Free Trade Agreement between the USA and Canada, over 70 percent of US exports to Canada were already duty free. The

FTA and then NAFTA began gradually eliminating the remaining tariffs. This elimination was, and still is, being done in four stages for specific products. The stages are:

- ◆ Immediately after the agreement took effect, which was January 1, 1994;
- ◆ Over a five-year period from 1994 to 1998 at the rate of 20 percent reduction per year;
- ◆ Over a ten-year period from 1994 to 2003 at the rate of 10 percent reduction per year; and
- ◆ Over a 15-year period from 1994 to 2008.

The list of remaining tariffs varies between the countries. For example, the US list of tariffs that are applied to commodities entering the USA from Canada is different to the list of tariffs applied to commodities coming in from Mexico. Canada and Mexico have similar but different lists. These lists are gradually reducing in size, and will be totally eliminated by the year 2008. A menu of NAFTA tariff rates by HS number is available at any US Trade Information Center, or you can contact the Census Bureau Foreign Trade Division at (301) 457-3047.

3. Rules of Origin

The origin of a commodity is the most important issue with regard to NAFTA, and the Certificate of Origin is the most important document associated with any cross-border activity. NAFTA, and earlier the FTA, has a clearly defined set of rules to establish the country of origin of each commodity. US Department of Commerce document STR920300 entitled *Canada-Export Procedures under the Free Trade Agreement* lists the goods that are defined as being wholly obtained or produced in the United States and/or Canada. The definitions, reproduced below, also apply to NAFTA:

1. Mineral goods extracted in the United States and/or Canada;
2. Goods harvested in the United States and/or Canada;
3. Live animals born and raised in the United States and/or Canada;
4. Goods such as fish, shellfish, and other marine life taken from the sea by a vessel registered or recorded with Canada or the United States that flies the flag of Canada or the United States;

5. Goods produced on board a factory vessel from goods referred to in (4) where the vessel is registered or recorded with Canada or the United States and flies the flag of Canada or the United States;

6. Goods taken by Canada, the United States, or a national of either country from or beneath the seabed outside the territorial sea of Canada or the territorial waters of the United States, where Canada or the United States has the right to exploit the seabed or the area beneath the seabed;

7. Goods taken from space where the goods are obtained by Canada, or the United States, or a national of either country, and not processed by a third country;

8. Waste and scrap that are derived in the United States or Canada from manufacturing operations and are used goods, where the wastes, scrap, and used goods are collected in the United States or Canada and are fit only for the recovery of raw materials; and

9. Goods produced in the United States or Canada exclusively from goods referred to in (1) to (8) or from their derivatives, at any stage of production.

The rules also apply to commodities that have portions originating in other countries, prior to being processed in a NAFTA country. For example, teak furniture manufactured in the USA is made with teak wood from another country. The rules of origin allow for the calculation of the portion that is of US origin, or the Regional Value Content (RVC). There are two ways of calculating the RVC: the transaction value method and the net cost method. Both of these are described in the figure below:

Calculation of Regional Value Content (RVC)

Transaction Value Method

This method is based on the price at which you sell the item. From this selling price, or transaction value, you subtract the value of non-North American materials, and divide the result by the selling price. Here is the method in mathematical form:

$$\frac{(\text{Selling Price}) - (\text{Value of Non-North American Material})}{\text{Selling Price}} = \text{Percentage of RVC}$$

Calculation of Regional Value Content (RVC)

Net Cost Method

This method is based on the cost of the product. From the total cost of the product you subtract all your costs (including royalties, shipping, marketing, etc.) and also the value of the non-North American materials. Then you divide the result by the total costs less all your costs. Here is the method in mathematical form:

$$\frac{(\text{Total Costs}) - (\text{Your Costs}) - (\text{Cost of Non-North American Materials})}{(\text{Total Costs}) - (\text{Your Costs})} = \%\ \text{RVC}$$

The Certificate of Origin is the document that describes the goods being exported. In addition to filling in details such as the names and addresses of the exporter and importer, you also have to provide a description of the goods, the HS tariff classification number, and the country of origin. See Sample 1, Certificate of Origin.

4. Business Travel

NAFTA makes it easier for cross-border movement of businesspersons who are citizens of the member countries. However, it does not change the immigration requirements of the three countries. A good explanation of the NAFTA Cross-Border Movement provisions is given in a pamphlet produced by the Canadian Department of Foreign Affairs and International Trade, entitled *Cross-Border Movement and the North American Free Trade Agreement*. Much of the information in this section is extracted from the pamphlet. It can be obtained on the Internet at <www.infoexport.gc.ca/nafta/cross-border/16006-e.asp>. Under NAFTA, there are four categories of business travelers:

 * Business visitors
 * Professionals
 * Intra-company transferees
 * Traders and investors

Business travelers may temporarily import certain goods duty-free, if the goods are associated with their activities. Goods allowed include —

 * professional equipment or tools of the trade;
 * equipment for the press, radio, or television broadcasters;

Sample 1
Certificate of Origin

DEPARTMENT OF THE TREASURY
UNITED STATES CUSTOMS SERVICE

OMB No. 1515-0204
See back of form for
Paperwork Reduction
Act Notice.

NORTH AMERICAN FREE TRADE AGREEMENT
CERTIFICATE OF ORIGIN

Please print or type   19 CFR 181.11, 181.22

1. EXPORTER NAME AND ADDRESS	2. BLANKET PERIOD (DD/MM/YY)
TAX IDENTIFICATION NUMBER:	FROM TO
3. PRODUCER NAME AND ADDRESS	4. IMPORTER NAME AND ADDRESS
TAX IDENTIFICATION NUMBER:	TAX IDENTIFICATION NUMBER:

5. DESCRIPTION OF GOOD(S)	6. HS TARIFF CLASSIFICATION NUMBER	7. PREFERENCE CRITERION	8. PRODUCER	9. NET COST	10. COUNTRY OF ORIGIN

I CERTIFY THAT:

· THE INFORMATION ON THIS DOCUMENT IS TRUE AND ACCURATE AND I ASSUME THE RESPONSIBILITY FOR PROVING SUCH REPRESENTATIONS. I UNDERSTAND THAT I AM LIABLE FOR ANY FALSE STATEMENTS OR MATERIAL OMISSIONS MADE ON OR IN CONNECTION WITH THIS DOCUMENT;

· I AGREE TO MAINTAIN, AND PRESENT UPON REQUEST, DOCUMENTATION NECESSARY TO SUPPORT THIS CERTIFICATE, AND TO INFORM, IN WRITING, ALL PERSONS TO WHOM THE CERTIFICATE WAS GIVEN OF ANY CHANGES THAT COULD AFFECT THE ACCURACY OR VALIDITY OF THIS CERTIFICATE;

· THE GOODS ORIGINATED IN THE TERRITORY OF ONE OR MORE OF THE PARTIES, AND COMPLY WITH THE ORIGIN REQUIREMENTS SPECIFIED FOR THOSE GOODS IN THE NORTH AMERICAN FREE TRADE AGREEMENT, AND UNLESS SPECIFICALLY EXEMPTED IN ARTICLE 411 OR ANNEX 401, THERE HAS BEEN NO FURTHER PRODUCTION OR ANY OTHER OPERATION OUTSIDE THE TERRITORIES OF THE PARTIES; AND

· THIS CERTIFICATE CONSISTS OF _____ PAGES, INCLUDING ALL ATTACHMENTS.

11.	11a. AUTHORIZED SIGNATURE		11b. COMPANY	
	11c. NAME *(Print or type)*		11d. TITLE	
	11e. DATE *(DD/MM/YY)*	11f. TELEPHONE > NUMBER	*(Voice)*	*(Facsimile)*

Customs Form 434 (040397)

- cinematographic equipment;
- sports equipment;
- goods for display and demonstration;
- commercial samples;
- advertising films; and
- printed advertising materials such as brochures, pamphlets, and catalogues.

5. Business Visitors

Business visitors are those businesspersons who plan to carry on any business activity related to research and design, growth, manufacturing and production, marketing, sales and distribution, after sales service, and general service. You qualify as a business visitor if —

- you are a citizen of a member country;
- you are seeking entry for business purposes;
- the proposed business activity is international in scope;
- you have no intention of entering the labor market;
- your primary source of remuneration is outside the country in which you are seeking entry;
- the principal place of business and the accrued profits remain outside of the country to which you are seeking entry; and
- you meet existing immigration requirements for temporary entry.

Business visitors to Canada must meet the general requirements listed above. Generally, no immigration document is issued to a business visitor. However, if terms and conditions are imposed on your entry, you will be issued a visitor record. A visitor record can be useful for frequent cross-border entries into Canada, or for extended stays. For example, after-sales personnel will be issued a visitor record if the intended stay is to be longer than two days.

After-sales service visits are defined as those "to install, repair or service, or supervise these functions, or to train workers to perform services, pursuant to a warranty or service contract entered into as an integral part of the sale of commercial or industrial equipment, machinery, or computer software purchased from an enterprise located outside of the country where the service is to be provided." The personnel involved must possess special knowledge essential to the contract requirements.

5.1 Professionals

Professionals are exempt from the usual process normally required to enter a foreign country's labor market. To qualify as a professional under NAFTA, you must meet the following criteria:

- ♦ You are a citizen of a member country.
- ♦ You are to be engaged in an occupation that is listed in the NAFTA Appendix 1603.D.1 (Appendix A of this book reproduces the NAFTA Appendix 1603.D.1, which includes the educational qualifications associated with the professions).
- ♦ You are qualified to work in the occupation in which you will be engaged.
- ♦ You have pre-arranged employment or a contractual agreement with an entity located within the country to which you are seeking temporary entry.
- ♦ You meet existing immigration requirements for temporary entry.

You will have to provide documentation that indicates —

- ♦ the professional activity to be carried out;
- ♦ the title of your job;
- ♦ a summary of your job duties;
- ♦ the start date and anticipated temporary length of stay; and
- ♦ the arrangement for remuneration.

The documentation can be in the form of —

- ♦ a signed contract between you and an enterprise; or
- ♦ a letter from your prospective employer(s) confirming that employment has been offered and accepted; or
- ♦ a letter from your present employer confirming that you are entering the member country in order to render professional services pursuant to a signed contract between your employer and an enterprise located within the country to which entry is being sought. (An enterprise can be an individual.)

In addition to the documentation listed above, you will have to demonstrate your professional qualification, usually with a certified copy of your education credentials. Your proof of citizenship can be shown with your passport. You may also have to prove to the immigration officers that you do not plan to indefinitely reside in the country to which you are seeking entry.

Once you have all the documentation required, you can apply for an Employment Authorization (IMM1295) at any Canadian embassy, consulate, or port of entry. The processing fee is $125 Canadian. After you have been admitted into Canada, you should obtain a Social Insurance Number or SIN, which is similar to the US Social Security Number. This can be obtained from any local Canada Employment Centre.

5.2 Intra-Company Transferees

Intra-company transferees are businesspersons employed by an enterprise who are seeking to provide services to a branch, parent, subsidiary, or affiliate of that enterprise, in a managerial or executive capacity, or in a manner that involves specialized knowledge. To qualify as an intra-company transferee you must —

- ◆ be a citizen of a member country;
- ◆ be seeking employment in an executive or managerial capacity, or one involving specialized knowledge;
- ◆ have been engaged in a similar position within the enterprise for at least one year within the previous three years;
- ◆ be transferring to an enterprise that has a clear relationship with the enterprise in which you are currently employed; and
- ◆ comply with existing immigration requirements for temporary entry.

You can apply for an Employment Authorization (IMM1295) at any Canadian embassy, consulate, or port of entry. The Employment Authorization is initially issued for periods of up to one year, but extensions may be granted in increments of up to two years. The processing fee is $125 Canadian. The documentation you require is —

- ◆ a detailed outline of the purpose and length of stay for which entry is being sought; and

- a detailed outline of your current job description, position title, and place in the organizational structure of the enterprise.

After you have been admitted into Canada, you should obtain a Social Insurance Number, or SIN, which is similar to the US Social Security Number. This can be obtained from any local Canada Employment Centre.

5.3 Traders and Investors

Traders are businesspersons who trade in goods and services between their country of residence and the country to which entry is being sought. To qualify as a trader you must prove that —

- you are a citizen of a member country;
- the enterprise has the nationality of a member country (at least 50 percent owned by citizens of the country);
- your predominant activity is to carry on substantial trade (exchange, purchase, or sale) in goods or services, principally between your present country of residence and the country to which you are seeking entry;
- the capacity in which you will be acting is executive or supervisory in nature or involves essential skills; and
- you otherwise meet existing immigration requirements for temporary entry.

Investors are businesspeople seeking to establish, develop, administer, or provide advice or key technical services to the operation of an investment to which a substantial amount of capital has been committed or is in the process of being committed. To qualify as an investor you must prove that —

- you are a citizen of a member country;
- the enterprise has the nationality of a member country (at least 50 percent owned by citizens of the country);
- substantial investment has or is being made;
- the investment is more than a marginal one;
- the enterprise is a real and operating commercial enterprise that operates continuously to produce some service or commodity for profit;

◆ you are in a position to develop and direct the enterprise; or if an employee of an investor, you are in a position that is executive, supervisory, or involves essential skills; and

◆ you comply with existing immigration requirements for temporary entry.

As a trader or investor you can apply for an Employment Authorization (IMM1295) at any Canadian embassy or consulate. The processing fee is $125 Canadian. You will also be required to provide information on your business by completing an Application for Trader/Investor Status. After you have been admitted to Canada, you should obtain a Social Insurance Number, or SIN, which is similar to the US Social Security Number. This can be obtained from any local Canada Employment Centre.

6. Settling Trade Disputes

NAFTA has a carefully defined dispute settlement process. Under NAFTA, a Free Trade Commission is set up that has a senior trade representative or designated alternate from each member country. Supporting the commission is a permanent secretariat with offices in each country. The secretariat attempts to avoid disputes or solve them through consultation. When this fails, the issue is raised to the level of the commission itself.

The commission members can call for an arbitration panel to be set up to resolve the dispute. The panels are made up of five members chosen from a list of professionals that has been approved by all member countries. The panel can call on experts for assistance in making the decision. The procedures are conducted under strict deadlines to ensure that disputes are settled as quickly as possible.

7. Additional Information

1. US Department of Commerce. Telephone (202) 482-2000.

2. Canadian Department of Foreign Affairs and International Trade, Services Policy Division. Telephone (613) 944-5047 or fax (613) 944-0058.

3. Industry Canada STRATEGIS Web site: http://strategis.ic.gc.ca

4. For HS numbers, contact the US Census Bureau Foreign Trade Division. Telephone (301) 457-3047.

5. US Department of Commerce document STR920300 entitled *Canada-Export Procedures under the Free Trade Agreement*.

6. Canadian Department of Foreign Affairs and International Trade pamphlet entitled *Cross-Border Movement and the North American Free Trade Agreement*. Available on the Internet: www.infoexport.gc.ca/nafta/cross-border/16006-e.asp

6
CONSUMER PROFILES

In many ways the Canadian consumer profiles are a reflection of those of the USA. They have been well-researched and documented, and are not the subject of this book. This chapter will provide some consumer profile information that should be of use from an export point of view. Additional information may be obtained from the Canadian Department of Foreign Affairs and International Trade, from where much of the information in this chapter was obtained. There are also many marketing consultant agencies in Canada that will provide more specific information for your particular product.

1. The Canadian Market

The population of Canada is about 30 million, and is highly urbanized. (Please see chapter 2 for more population details.) About 90 percent of Canadians live close to the Canada-USA border, and the majority live in the two large provinces of Ontario and Quebec. The following table shows the population and Gross Domestic Product (GDP) of the various regions and provinces of Canada:

Regional/Provincial Population and GDP

Region/Province	Population	Percent of Population	Percent of GDP
Atlantic Canada	2,409,000	8.1	6.0
Newfoundland	575,000	1.9	1.3
Prince Edward Island	136,000	0.4	0.3
Nova Scotia	938,000	3.2	2.4
New Brunswick	760,000	2.6	2.0
Central Canada	18,080,000	62.3	61.8
Quebec	7,334,000	24.8	22.4
Ontario	10,746,000	37.5	40.4
Western Canada	8,667,000	29.3	30.7
Manitoba	1,138,000	3.8	3.4
Saskatchewan	1,016,000	3.4	3.1
Alberta	2,747,000	9.3	10.9
British Columbia	3,766,000	12.8	13.3
Northern Territories	96,000	0.3	0.4
Yukon	30,000	0.1	0.1
Northwest Territories[1]	66,000	0.2	0.3

Note: 1. In 1999, the Northwest Territories were divided into two territories: Nunavut and the remaining area, which as yet is still named the Northwest Territory.

Atlantic Canada has suffered recently from the decline of the fishing industry, a mainstay of the region. However, tourism has become an important industry, along with the petroleum industry. Halifax is the main port on the east coast of Canada. The Newfoundland economy, though still very uncertain, should benefit from major new mining developments and offshore oil production.

Central Canada is the industrial powerhouse of Canada. The province of Ontario itself is the USA's second largest trading partner. The automobile assembly and parts industries of southern Ontario export more vehicles to the USA than do all other countries combined. Toronto has developed into a major financial center. Ottawa, in addition to being the capital of Canada, has developed world class high-technology industries that export all over the world. The province of Quebec boasts a significant and expanding aerospace industry that also exports its products throughout the world.

Western Canada, in particular the three prairie provinces, is the breadbasket of Canada. The oil and gas industry, located mainly in Alberta, has become a major economic factor. Calgary also has a rapidly developing high-tech industry. British Columbia is rich in forestry, mining, and fishing, and has a quickly growing high-tech industry. The port of Vancouver is the busiest port in Canada.

The Northern Territories, though sparse in population, are rich in mineral resources and also boast a thriving tourist industry.

2. Canadian Incomes

The average Canadian family income in 1995 was $54,200 Canadian, or about $35,000 US. The table below, provided by Statistics Canada, shows the sources of Canadian income.

Sources of Canadian Income

Source	Amount ($Billions CDN)	Percent of Total
Labor	422	63.5
Farm	2	0.2
Unincorporated Business	42	6.3
Interest and Investment	86	13.0
Government (pensions, etc.)	113	17.0

The average personal income per capita was $22,611 Canadian, or about $15,000 US in 1995, and it varies from province to province. Like the USA, the typical Canadian family has more than one income earner. Fifty-seven percent of Canadian women are now in the labor force. The disposable income of Canadians (their personal income minus taxes) has been increasing slowly. But Canada remains a highly taxed country.

3. Expenditure Patterns

Canadians spend about $500 billion a year on goods and services. Like the USA, the services now account for more than half of the household expenditures. Also like the USA, there has been a rapid rise in spending on information technologies. About one-third of Canadian households have a computer, and about 40 percent of those computers are connected to the Internet. The table below, provided by Statistics Canada, shows the distribution of Canadian personal expenditures on goods and services in 1995:

Canadian Expenditures on Goods and Services

Category	% Personal Expenditure
Durable Goods	14.7
Motor Vehicles	6.9
Furniture and Appliances	2.7
Other	5.1
Semi-Durable Goods	9.1
Clothing and Footwear	5.1
Other	4.0
Non-Durable Goods	25.8
Food	11.0
Motor Fuel	3.1
Electricity and Other Fuel	3.3
Other	8.4
Services	50.4
Rent and Mortgage	20.4
Restaurants and Hotels	5.9
Expenditure Abroad	0.3
Other	23.8

There are more than eleven million individual households in Canada, and about two-thirds of them are owner-occupied homes. The following table, from Statistics Canada, shows the percentage of Canadian household ownership of various products:

Canadian Household Ownership of Products

Product	% Households Owning
Automobile	74.5
Truck or Van	30.8
Telephone	98.5
Cellular Phone	14.1
Cable Television	74.0
CD Player	53.4
Home Computer	31.6
Refrigerator	99.7
Microwave Oven	83.4
Dishwasher	47.1
Air Conditioner	27.6

4. Multiculturalism

Canada has two official languages (English and French) as well as a large Aboriginal population. There is also a significant and increasing portion of the Canadian population that claims other than these three ethnic origins. (Please see chapter 3 for more information on cultural backgrounds.) The following table, from Statistics Canada, shows the numbers of Canadians that reported other ethnic origins in the 1991 census:

Ethnic Origins Other Than British, French, or Aboriginal

Ethnic Origin	At Least One Ancestor
German	2,793,780
Italian	1,147,775

Ethnic Origin	At Least One Ancestor
Ukrainian	1,054,295
Dutch	966,595
Polish	740,710
Scandinavian	717,200
Chinese	652,645
South Asian	488,370
Caribbean	305,290
Portuguese	292,185
Hungarian	213,700
Balkan	198,650
Arab	194,880
Greek	191,480

5. Additional Information

1. Canadian Department of Foreign Affairs and International Trade Internet site: www.dfait-maeci.gc.ca.

2. Industry Canada STRATEGIS Web site: http://strategis.ic.gc.ca.

3. *Canada Year Book*, Statistics Canada, Ottawa, Canada, 1997.

7
LABELING, REGULATIONS, AND STANDARDS

Like most countries, Canada has laws and regulations intended to protect the consumer. These differ in varying degrees from those of the USA, and you must ensure that your product complies with them. The main laws are —

- ♦ the Food and Drugs Act,
- ♦ the Consumer Packaging and Labelling Act,
- ♦ the Competition Act, and
- ♦ the Weights and Measures Act.

The regulations associated with these acts are briefly explained in this chapter. More detailed information is available on the Internet at the Industry Canada home page, <www.ic.gc.ca>, from where much of the following information was obtained. The Canadian Standards Association (CSA) is also discussed in this chapter.

1. Food Labeling

Food labeling is probably the most difficult labeling you will face as an exporter to Canada. If your product is not a food or drug, you may want to skip this section and go directly to the following sections on non-food labeling and textile labeling. Food labeling is the responsibility of the Canadian Food Inspection Agency (CFIA), which has published the *Guide to Food Labelling and Advertising*. It is available in print or disk format from CFIA by calling (613) 225-2342, or on the Internet at <www.cfia-acia.agr.ca>. Much of the information in this section is extracted from the guide, and the main topics are covered in order to give you an idea of what you must consider before you export food to Canada. However, it is recommended that you obtain a copy of the guide and study it in more detail before taking any action to alter your current labeling.

A label is required on all prepackaged products, with a few exceptions. The definition of a prepackaged product is "any food that is contained in a package in the manner in which it is ordinarily sold to, used by, or purchased by a consumer or by a commercial enterprise, without being repackaged." The exceptions are —

- ♦ one-bite confections, such as candy or a stick of chewing gum, sold individually; and
- ♦ fresh fruits or vegetables packaged in a wrapper or confining band of less than ½ inch (12.7 mm).

All mandatory information must be included in both official languages (English and French), except the dealer's name and address, which can appear in either language. The province of Quebec has additional requirements concerning the use of French language on all products marketed within the province. Information on these requirements may be obtained from —

Ministere de l'Agriculture, des Pecheries et de l'Alimentation du Quebec
200, Chemin Sainte-Foy
Quebec, Quebec   G1R 4X6
Telephone: (418) 380-2110
Toll free: 1-888-222-6272

Net quantity must be declared on the label, with some exceptions. The type height must be a minimum 1.6 mm, based on the height of the lowercase letter 'o'. The net quantity must be declared in metric units on the principal display panel on consumer packages —

- by volume, for liquids (in milliliters, or liters for amounts over 1000 ml);
- by weight, for solids (in grams, or kilograms for amounts over 1000g); and
- by count, for certain foods such as eggs.

American units of measure may also be used on labels, provided an appropriate and accurate metric net quantity is declared. US fluid measures, such as gallons, are smaller than Canadian measures and must be identified as 'US' on the label. An exception is the US fluid ounce, which is slightly larger than the Canadian fluid ounce (1 fl. oz. US = 1.041 fl. oz. Canadian), and, if shown, does not need to be identified as US.

Prepackaged multi-ingredient foods must have an ingredient list in descending order of proportion by weight in the food. Spices, seasonings, natural and artificial flavors, flavor enhancers, food additives, and vitamin and mineral nutrients may be shown at the end of the list in any order. There are some exceptions to the ingredient list requirement. And, of course, the ingredient list must be in English and French.

A durable life date ('best before' date) is required on prepackaged foods with a durable life of 90 days or less. The durable life is "the period, starting on the day a food is packaged for retail sale, that the food will retain its normal wholesomeness, palatability and nutritional value, when it is stored under conditions appropriate for that product." The following are exceptions to the durable life date requirement:

- Prepackaged fresh fruits and vegetables
- Prepackaged individual portions of food served with meals or snacks, by restaurants, airlines, etc.
- Prepackaged individual servings of food prepared by a commissary and sold in automatic vending machines or mobile canteens
- Prepackaged donuts

Container sizes must be standardized for certain food prepackaged for sale to consumers:

- Biscuits or cookies:
    - Less than or equal to 75 grams: net quantity of product that is a multiple of 1 gram.
    - 100 to 300 grams: multiples of 25 grams.
    - 350 to 500 grams: multiples of 50 grams.
    - 600 grams to 1 kilogram: multiples of 100 grams.
    - 1.25 kilograms or more: multiples of 250 grams.
- Wine:
    - 50, 100, 200, 250, 375, 500, or 750 milliliters.
    - 1, 1.5, 2, 3, or 4 liters.
- Glucose syrup and refined sugar syrup:
    - 125, 250, 375, 500, or 750 milliliters.
    - 1 or 1.5 liters.
    - More than 1.5 liters: multiples of 1 liter.
- Peanut butter:
    - 250, 375, 500, 750 grams.
    - 1, 1.5, 2 kilograms.

2. Non-Food Labeling

The packaging and labeling of non-food products at all levels of trade comes under the Consumer Packaging and Labelling Act. (Canadians spell labeling with two 'l's.) The act defines three mandatory requirements:

- Product identity
- Product net quantity
- Dealer's name and principal place of business

The information must be included in both official languages (English and French), except the dealer's name and address, which can appear in either language. The province of Quebec has additional requirements concerning the use of French language on all products marketed within the province. Information on these requirements may be obtained from —

Office de la langue francaise
800 Tour de la Place Victoria
Montreal, Quebec H4Z 1G8
Telephone: (514) 873-6565
Fax: (514) 873-3488

Certain products are exempt from the Consumer Packaging and Labelling Act regulations. Some of these are —

♦ drugs and medical devices;

♦ commercial-, industrial-, or institutional-use only products;

♦ products for export only;

♦ products sold only to a duty-free store;

♦ prepackaged textile articles;

♦ replacement parts for consumer durables (cars, appliances) if not displayed to consumers; and

♦ certain artists' supplies.

Pet food products come under the Consumer Packaging and Labelling Act. Prepackaged agricultural products such as feeds, seeds, fertilizers, and pest-control products do not come under the Consumer Packaging and Labelling Act, but are regulated by Agriculture and Agri-Food Canada. Cosmetics come under both the Consumer Packaging and Labelling Act and the Food and Drugs Act, which is regulated by Health Canada. Test-market products may be exempted for up to one year from bilingual labeling and standardization of container sizes. To qualify for this exemption —

♦ the product must not have been previously sold in Canada;

♦ the product must differ substantially from any other sold in Canada with respect to composition, function, state, or packaging form; and

♦ the existing labeling on the product must comply with the detailed requirements of the law, except for bilingual labeling and container standardization.

3. Textile Labeling

Consumer textile articles come under the Textile Labelling Act, the Textile Labelling and Advertising Regulations, and the Canada Care Labelling Program. Industry Canada carries out inspections to ensure that regulations are being met. They also provide a number of labeling-related publications on the Internet at <http://strategis.ic .gc.ca/fbp>. In general, the following must have a label with information on fiber content and dealer identity:

- ♦ Clothing
- ♦ Carpets
- ♦ Upholstered furniture coverings
- ♦ Bedding
- ♦ Fabrics sold by the meter
- ♦ Other household textiles

There are a number of consumer textile articles that are exempt from the labeling requirements. Examples of these are —

- ♦ articles intended for a one-time use only;
- ♦ overshoes, boots, shoes, indoor slippers, footwear liners, and insoles;
- ♦ handbags, luggage, carrying cases, brushes;
- ♦ toys, ornaments, pictures, lamp shades, tapestries, wall hangings, wall coverings, room dividers, screens, book covers, book marks, gift wrap, flags, and pennants;
- ♦ sports and games equipment other than sports garments;
- ♦ lawn and beach furniture, including lawn and beach umbrellas and parasols, and hammocks;
- ♦ playpens, crib-pens, strollers, jumpers, walkers, and car seats for infants or children;
- ♦ labels, adhesive tapes and sheets, cleaning cloths, wipers, therapeutic devices, and heating pads;
- ♦ pet accessories;
- ♦ belts, suspenders, armbands, garters, sanitary belts, and bandages;
- ♦ curler head covers, hair nets, and shower caps;

- carpet underpadding;
- musical instruments and accessories;
- straw or felt headwear;
- padding or helmets worn in sports;
- non-fibrous materials that do not have a fabric support, including films and foams;
- household twine, string, craft ribbon not intended to be used in the construction of prescribed consumer textile articles, baler twine, binder twine, and gift wrap ribbon; and
- items which are exported, or sold to or by a duty-free store.

Care labeling is voluntary under the Canada Care Labelling Program. It is based on five basic symbols, although words in both English and French may be used. The symbols provide information on washing, bleaching, drying, ironing, and dry cleaning the article. They relate to the following properties of textiles:

- Colorfastness
- Dimensional stability
- Effect of retained chlorine (bleach)
- Maximum safe ironing temperature

4. Environmental Labeling and Advertising

The Consumer Packaging and Labelling Act also regulates the environmental impact of consumer products. The main concern is the correct use of the terms, such as —

- degradable,
- compostable,
- post-use,
- recyclable, and
- recycled content.

5. Food Inspection

Canadian laws and regulations that protect human, animal, and plant health are enforced by the Canadian Food Inspection Agency (CFIA). The CFIA monitors imports into the country to ensure that all imports meet the standards set for consumption in Canada (the CFIA also monitors exports from Canada). The range of products inspected by the CFIA is too wide to attempt to explain in this publication. If your product is related to human, animal, or plant health, contact the CFIA at their Internet site, <www.cfia-acia.agr.ca>, or at —

Canadian Food Inspection Agency
59 Camelot Drive
Nepean, Ontario K1A 0Y9
Telephone: (613) 225-2342

6. The Competition Act

The Competition Act governs how business is to be done in Canada. It applies to all those doing business in Canada, and covers both criminal law offenses as well as civil law issues. The following criminal offenses are covered by the Act:

- Price fixing or conspiracy to fix prices, which may occur when business competitors agree on prices
- Bid-rigging, in which one or more bidders agree to arrange and submit bids
- Misleading advertising that is materially misleading

Civil law matters are decided by the Competition Tribunal. The main civil law issues covered by the Act are —

- abuse of dominant position to lessen competition;
- exclusive dealing requirements placed on a customer by a supplier to prevent the customer from dealing with another product;
- refusal to deal with a customer, thus preventing him or her from obtaining adequate supplies of a product; and
- mergers by one or more businesses.

7. Advertising Regulations

Under the Competition Act, it is a criminal offense to engage in certain kinds of misleading advertising and deceptive marketing practices. Misleading advertising is a representation made to the public that is materially misleading; that is, it influences the consumer to buy for misleading reasons. Deceptive marketing practices include —

- representations that are false or misleading;
- performance claims that are not based on proper and adequate tests;
- misleading warranties or guarantees;
- false or misleading representations of tests and testimonials;
- inflated regular or ordinary prices;
- double-ticketing;
- pyramid-selling and multilevel marketing;
- referral-selling;
- sale above advertised price;
- promotional contests; and
- bait and switch advertising.

The following advertising "dos and don'ts" are provided by Industry Canada at their Web site, <http://strategis.ic.gc.ca/SSG /ct01072e.html>:

- Do avoid fine-print disclaimers. They often fail to change the general impression conveyed by an advertisement. If you do use them, make sure the overall impression created by the ad and the disclaimer is not misleading.
- Do fully and clearly disclose all material information in the advertisement.
- Do avoid using terms or phrases in an advertisement that are not meaningful and clear to the ordinary person.
- Do remember that the public includes the ignorant and credulous as well as the knowledgeable and sophisticated.
- Do charge the lowest of two or more prices appearing on products.
- Do ensure that you have reasonable quantities of a product advertised at a bargain price.
- Do, when conducting a contest, disclose all material details required by the Act before potential participants are committed to it.

- Do ensure that your sales force is familiar with these "dos and don'ts." Advertisers may be held responsible for representations made by employees.

- Don't confuse "regular price" with "manufacturer's suggested listed price," or a like term. They are often not the same.

- Don't use "regular price" in an advertisement unless it is the price at which the product is usually sold.

- Don't use the words "sale" or "special" in relation to the price of a product unless a significant price reduction has occurred.

- Don't run a "sale" for a long period or repeat it every week.

- Don't increase the price of a product or service to cover the cost of a "free" product or service.

- Don't use illustrations that are different from the product being sold.

- Don't make a performance claim before you can prove it, even if you think it is accurate. Testimonials usually don't amount to adequate proof.

- Don't sell a product above your advertised price.

- Don't unduly delay the distribution of prizes when conducting a contest.

- Don't forget that no one actually needs to be misled for a court to find that an advertisement is misleading.

- Don't forget that ignorance and/or lack of intent are not valid defenses.

8. Weights and Measures

If your business in Canada involves measurement standards, devices associated with measurement, or goods and services that are traded on the basis of measurement, you will be subject to the Weights and Measures Act. It requires that —

- commodities and services that are traded on the basis of measurement be accurate within prescribed limits;

- only legal-for-trade units of measurement are used in trade;

- device designs be approved;

- only approved devices are used in trade;

- all devices be inspected and certified before trade use commences; and

- weighing and measuring devices used in trade are accurate within prescribed limits and are not used in a fraudulent manner.

Chapter 4 gives detailed information on the International System of Units (SI), or metric system, which is used in Canada. Additional information on the Weights and Measures Act, including the fees charged for inspection services, is available on the Internet at the Measurement Canada site, <http://strategis.ic.gc.ca/sc_mrksv /meascan/engdoc/homepage.html>.

9. Canadian Standards Association

The Canadian Standards Association (CSA) is Canada's largest standards development and certification organization. It is an independent, non-government, non-profit association involved in the certification of a number of product areas such as —

- appliances — motor operated
- fuel-burning equipment
- hazardous locations
- heating and air conditioning
- home entertainment
- industrial controls
- information technology
- lighting products
- metrology
- mobile homes and recreational vehicles

Occupational health and safety:

- medical and laboratory equipment
- mechanical and plumbing products
- power supplies
- process control
- sensing and signaling equipment
- switchgear

- ◆ telecommunication
- ◆ wire and cable
- ◆ wiring devices

CSA standards are developed and written by volunteer committees representing a combination of government, industry, academia, special interest groups, consumer groups, and the public. All CSA standards are living documents, monitored and updated by the committees when necessary to respond to new industry needs and technologies. While CSA standards are voluntary, they frequently form the basis for government legislation.

CSA certification tells people that a product or system has been evaluated under a formal system of examination, testing, and inspection, and that it complies with applicable standards. Certification is mandatory in order to market electrical products in Canada, and the sale of electrical products is governed by provincial legislation. The CSA certification mark shows that the product is certified.

CSA works with a world-wide network of partner agencies, including US agencies. If your product has been certified by a US agency, it may also be considered to have CSA approval. You can get more information on the CSA at their Web site, <www.csa.ca>, from where much of this information has been gathered, or you can contact them at —

Canadian Standards Association
Central Office
178 Rexdale Boulevard
Etobicoke (Toronto), Ontario M9W 1R3
Telephone: 1-800-463-6727 or (416) 747-4000

10. Additional Information

1. *Guide to Food Labelling and Advertising*, available from Canadian Food Inspection Agency at their Internet site, <www.cfia-acia.agr.ca>, or write to them at Canadian Food Inspection Agency, 59 Camelot Drive, Nepean, Ontario, K1A 0Y9, Telephone: (613) 225-2342

2. For information on food labeling in the province of Quebec, contact Ministere de l'Agriculture, des Pecheries et de l'Alimentation du Quebec, 200-A Chemin Sainte-Foy,

Quebec, Quebec, G1R 4X6, Telephone: (418) 380-2110, Toll-free: 1-888-222-6272

3. For information on non-food labeling in the province of Quebec, contact Office de la langue francaise, 800 Tour de la Place Victoria, Montreal, Quebec, H4Z 1G8,
Telephone: (514) 873-6565
Fax: (514) 873-3488

4. For clothing care information, contact Canada Care Labelling Program on the Internet:
www.strategis.ic.gc.ca/fbp

5. For advertising regulations and guidelines, contact Industry Canada on the Internet:
www.strategis.ic.gc.ca/SSG/dm01256e.html

6. For information on weights and measures, contact Measurement Canada on the Internet:
http://strategis.ic.gc.ca/sc_mrksv/meascan/engdoc/hompage.html

7. Canadian Standards Association, Central Office, 178 Rexdale Boulevard, Etobicoke, Ontario, M9W 1R3,
Telephone: 1-800-463-6727 or (416) 747-4000

8
INTELLECTUAL PROPERTY PROTECTION

Intellectual property laws of Canada are somewhat similar to those of the USA. This chapter explains some of the main features of Canadian intellectual property laws, and also discusses patent agents in Canada. However, readers are cautioned to seek appropriate legal advice on the subject if they require it. The use of patent agents, trademark agents, and similar professionals is also recommended.

1. Intellectual Property in Canada

Canada, like many countries, belongs to the Paris Convention for the Protection of Industrial Property. An important feature of the Paris Convention is the 'convention priority.' This means that your filing date in one country will be recognized by all the other countries, provided you file in those countries within a year of first filing. So if you file a patent application in the US on July 15, 2000, and if you file a similar application in Canada before July 15, 2001, the Canadian authorities will honor your US filing date of July 15, 2000. However, it is important to note that you must file for intellectual property protection in Canada (or any other country) as well as in the USA if you want the same protection you enjoy in the USA.

The Canadian Intellectual Property Office (CIPO), part of Industry Canada, is responsible for intellectual property rights in Canada. These include —

♦ patents,

♦ trade marks,

♦ copyright,

♦ industrial design, and

♦ integrated circuit topographies.

These various intellectual properties are often confused with each other. Some basic definitions will help to distinguish between them:

♦ Patents are for new technologies (processes, structures, and functions).

♦ A trademark is a word, symbol, or picture, or combination of these, used to distinguish the goods or services of one person or organization from those of another.

♦ Copyrights are for literary, artistic, dramatic, or musical works, as well as computer software.

♦ Industrial designs are for the shape, pattern, or ornamentation applied to an industrially produced object.

♦ "Integrated circuit topographies" refers to the three-dimensional configuration of the electronic circuits embodied in integrated circuit products or layout designs.

You can obtain more information on the subject of intellectual property protection from the CIPO site on the Internet at <http://cipo.gc.ca>, from where much of the information in this chapter was obtained.

2. Patents

In general, a patent in a country gives you the right to exclude others from making, using, or selling your invention for a period of time from the day the patent is granted. These rights extend throughout the country in which the patent is granted, but not to foreign countries. Even if you have a US patent on your invention, you will still have to get a Canadian patent for protection in Canada. In Canada, a patent is granted for up to 20 years from the date it is issued.

The Patent Cooperation Treaty (PCT), administered by the World Intellectual Property Organization based in Geneva, assists you in filing patents in other countries, including Canada. The PCT provides standardized international filing procedures, and under it you can file for a patent in up to 89 countries. You are also released from the one-year deadline for filing in other countries. Instead, you can file within the US, in English, and have up to 20 or 30 months to complete the application and pay the required fees. Contact the US Patent Office for more information on how you can make use of the PCT.

The Canadian Patent Office, a part of the CIPO, is responsible for all government patent activities. These include —

+ receiving and examining applications for patents,
+ granting patents to qualifying applicants,
+ recording assignments of patents,
+ selling copies of patents to the public, and
+ publishing and disseminating patent information.

To qualify for a patent in Canada, an invention must meet three basic criteria: it must be new, it must be useful, and it must be inventive and not obvious to someone skilled in the area. A patentable invention can be a product, a composition, an apparatus, a process, or an improvement on an existing patent. You cannot patent a scientific principle, an abstract theorem, a method of doing business, a computer program (see the copyright section in this chapter), or a medical treatment. You should not publicly disclose your invention in Canada prior to applying for a patent, because this may jeopardize your application. To obtain a patent in Canada you must go through the following steps:

1. Preliminary Search:

   You should first make sure that your invention has not been already patented, and this involves a search of existing patents. You can do this in a number of ways:

   ◆ Via the Canadian Patent Database on the Internet at the Industry Canada Strategis site <strategis.ic.gc.ca>

   ◆ At the Patent Office at Place du Portage I, 50 Victoria Street, Hull, Quebec K1A 0C9 (near Ottawa)

   ◆ Through the TechSource electronic patent system that records Canadian patents back to 1920. This service is available at the Patent Office.

2. Patent Application:

   A patent application consists of an abstract, a specification, and often drawings. The abstract is a brief summary of the contents of the specification. The specification has two parts: a clear and complete description of the invention and its usefulness; and claims that define the boundaries of the patent protection. The specification may be supported by drawings.

Patent searches and applications are very complex. It is therefore recommended that you use a Canadian patent agent for these procedures. (Please see section on agents in this chapter.)

3. Trademarks

A trademark is a word, symbol, design, or combination of these used to distinguish the goods or services of one person or organization from those of others. There are three basic categories of trademarks:

1. *Ordinary Marks*: Words or symbols, such as "Blue Camelion"

2. *Certification Marks*: Marks that identify goods or services that meet a defined standard, such as the "Wool Mark" owned by The Wool Bureau of Canada Limited

3. *Distinguishing Guise*: A unique shape of a product or its package; for example, beverages bottled in a distinguishingly shaped bottle

Registering your trademark gives you the legal title and exclusive use of it. In Canada, trademark registration is good for 15 years, and can be renewed for an additional 15 years. Registration is by the Trade-marks Office, which is part of the CIPO. The main functions of the Trade-marks Office are to —

♦ receive and examine applications for trademark registration;

♦ grant registrations to qualifying applicants;

♦ record and index registrations of trademarks;

♦ approve and record assignments of trademark applications;

♦ maintain records of trademark registrations and pending marks, and a search room of these records for public use;

♦ provide general information to the public about trademark registration process; and

♦ publish the *Trade-Marks Journal*.

To register a trademark, file an application with the Trade-marks Office and pay an initial non-refundable application fee of $150 Canadian. Your application will then go through an examination process to make sure that your mark meets all the requirements of the Trademarks Act. Your application will also be published in the *Trade-Marks Journal*, a weekly publication that informs others of applications and allows them to challenge these applications. If your application is successful, you are charged $200 Canadian for a certificate of registration. The Trade-marks Office is located at —

Trade-marks Office
50 Victoria Street
Place du Portage I, 2nd Floor
Hull, Quebec K1A 0C9 (near Ottawa)

Prior to the application, you should conduct a search of existing trademarks to ensure you are not infringing on an already registered trademark. This activity can be done at the Trade-marks Office, but it requires experience to do a proper search. For this reason, and because of the complexity required in the application, it is recommended that you use a Canadian trademark agent.

4. Copyright

As in the USA, when you create an original work in Canada, you automatically have copyright protection. This also applies to citizens of countries that are signatories to the Berne Convention or the Universal Copyright Convention, or a country that is a member of the World Trade Organization. Both Canada and the USA are signatories to all of these; as a citizen of the USA, you therefore have automatic copyright protection for your work in Canada. Only sound recordings are not covered under these copyright treaties. The copyright usually lasts for 50 years after the death of the author, except for photographs, cinematographs, and sound recordings, which are covered for 50 years after they were created. The following are covered under Canadian copyright law:

♦ Literary works, including books, pamphlets, poems, and other works consisting of text. (Not included is the idea for a plot or facts in an article.)

♦ Computer programs. (Not included is the name of a program, which could be protected through trademark laws.)

♦ Dramatic works, including films, videos, plays, screenplays, and scripts. (Not included is the method of staging a play.)

♦ Musical works, including compositions that consist of both words and music, or music only, with the lyrics falling into the literary works category. (Not included is the title of a song.)

♦ Artistic works, including paintings, drawings, maps, photographs, sculptures, and architectural works.

You do not have to register your copyright to have protection in Canada, but, as in the USA, it may be helpful to do so in the event of a legal dispute. When you register with the Copyright Office, you receive a certificate that proves your ownership. For information on copyright registration, contact —

Copyright Office
Canadian Intellectual Property Office
50 Victoria Street
Place du Portage I
Hull, Quebec K1A 0C9
Telephone: (819) 997-1936
Fax: (819) 953-7620
Email: cipo.contact@ic.gc.ca
Internet: http://cipo.gc.ca

5. Industrial Design

Industrial design is the features of shape, pattern, ornamentation, or configuration, or any combination thereof, applied to a finished article of manufacture. There are no reciprocal agreements between the USA and Canada (or other countries) in the protection of industrial designs. In Canada, however, the Industrial Design Act provides you with protection, and as a foreigner you are free to register your design in Canada. The advantage of registering is that you will have exclusive rights to your design for a period of ten years. Others are not legally allowed to make, import for trade or business, rent, or sell your design.

To qualify for registration, the design must have features that appeal to the eye. You can not register the following:

- Designs that are utilitarian only and which are not intended to provide visual appeal
- Designs that have no fixed appearance
- Designs for components that are not clearly visible
- A method of construction
- An idea
- Materials used in the construction of an article
- The useful function of the article
- The color

An application for industrial design registration is very complex, and it is recommended that you use a registered patent agent. (See the section on agents.) The application requires the following:

- A written description of the features of the design, emphasizing its visual aspects rather than its utilitarian aspects.
- Drawings or photographs of the design.
- A declaration that you are the owner of the design, and that, to your knowledge, no one else has used the design.
- A fee of $160 Canadian.

As a foreign applicant, you must provide the name and address of someone in Canada who will act as your representative.

You can obtain more information on industrial design protection in Canada from the Internet at the Industrial Design Office site,

<http://strategis.ic.gc.ca/sc_mrksv/cipo/id/id_guide-e.html>. You can also contact the Office at:

Industrial Design Office
Canadian Intellectual Property Office
50 Victoria Street
Hull, Quebec K1A 0C9
Telephone: (819) 997-1725

6. Integrated Circuit Topographies

Integrated circuits have become an integral part of many products, and like many countries, Canada has passed a law to protect the rights of the inventor or developer. The Integrated Circuit Topography Act came into force in 1993. The Act refers to the layers of semiconductors, metals, insulators, and other materials on a substrate that form the three-dimensional configuration. You should note that the Act allows others to reverse engineer the integrated circuit to design a new and original one. However, registration does exclude others from —

- ◆ reproducing a protected topography or any substantial part of one;

- ◆ manufacturing an integrated circuit component incorporating the topography or a substantial part of one;

- ◆ importing or commercially exploiting a registered topography or substantial part of one; and

- ◆ importing and commercially exploiting an industrial article that incorporates an integrated circuit that embodies a protected topography or a substantial part of one.

As a foreigner, you can also register a topography for protection. The protection lasts for ten years from the date of filing the application. It is recommended that you use a patent agent in Canada to help you with the application. For more information on registering, contact:

Integrated Circuit Topographies Office
Canadian Intellectual Property Office
50 Victoria Street
Hull, Quebec K1A 0C9
Telephone: (819) 997-1725

7. Plant Breeders' Rights

The Canadian Plant Breeders' Rights Act provides exclusive rights to developers of new varieties of some plants. The rights include your control of the multiplication and sale of the seed for up to 18 years. For more information on this subject, contact the Canadian Intellectual Properties Office, telephone (819) 997-1936.

8. Agents

The process of obtaining a patent is very complex, and it is highly recommended that you use a Canadian patent agent to assist you. Registered patent agents in Canada must pass rigorous examinations in patent law and practice before they may represent inventors at the Patent Office. A list of registered patent agents is kept in the Patent Office. Once you have appointed a patent agent, all correspondence with the Patent Office must be through the agent. Patent agents' fees are not regulated, and you should negotiate them before the patent application begins. To register an industrial design or an integrated circuit topography in Canada, it is also advised that you use a patent agent.

Applying for a trademark is also a complex task, and a registered trademark agent is recommended. The Trade-marks Office can provide you with a list of registered agents. They can be lawyers, notaries, or people who have worked in the field of trademark application for at least two years under the supervision of a registered agent and have passed a qualifying examination.

9. Additional Information

1. Canadian Intellectual Property Office Web site: http://cipo.gc.ca

2. US Patent and Trademark Office, Crystal Plaza 3, Room 2602, Washington, DC 20231
   Telephone: (703) 308-4357
   Toll free: 1-800-786-9199

3. Patent Office, Canadian Intellectual Property Office, Place du Portage I, 50 Victoria Street
   Hull, Quebec K1A 0C9
   Telephone: (819) 997-1936

4. Industry Canada Strategis Web site:
   www.strategis.ic.gc.ca

5. Trade-marks Office, Canadian Intellectual Property
   Office, Place du Portage I, 50 Victoria Street
   Hull, Quebec K1A 0C9
   Telephone: (819) 997-1936

6. Copyright Office, Canadian Intellectual Property Office,
   50 Victoria Street, Place du Portage I
   Hull, Quebec K1A 0C9
   Telephone: (819) 997-1936
   Fax: (819) 953-7620
   Email: cipo.contact@ic.gc.ca
   Web site: http://cipo.gc.ca

7. Industrial Design Office, Canadian Intellectual Property
   Office, 50 Victoria Street, Hull, Quebec K1A 0C9
   Telephone: (819) 997-1725
   Web site: http://strategis.ic.gc.ca/sc_mrksv/cipo/id
   /id_guide-e.html

8. Integrated Circuit Topographies Office, Canadian Intellectual Property Office, 50 Victoria Street
   Hull, Quebec K1A 0C9
   Telephone: (819) 997-1725

9
TRANSPORTATION AND COMMUNICATION

The Canadian population density averages only about eight people per square mile. To efficiently move people, goods, and data throughout this sparsely populated country requires modern and efficient transportation and communication systems. Canada has become a world leader in the development of these systems for domestic use, and also exports the technology throughout the world. If your product is for use in these industries, you should have an excellent market in Canada. This chapter provides information and statistics on the Canadian transportation and communication systems. Details on the associated business opportunities are provided in following chapters.

1. Road Transportation

Canada has more miles of road and railway track per person than most other countries, including the USA. The following table shows the amount of roadways in Canada:

Roadways in Canada	
Expressways	11,780 miles
Paved	210,410 miles
Unpaved	410,830 miles
Total	**633,020 miles**

Intercity passenger travel is about 7 billion passenger miles per year, or about 90 percent of all intercity trips. The majority of this is in private automobiles. Canada is second only to the USA in automobiles per person, averaging about one automobile for every two people. Intercity bus service is the largest public passenger service in Canada. There are more than 1000 operators serving over 3400 communities.

Canadian highways handle about 75 percent of the freight shipments in Canada. This amounts to almost 50 billion tonne-kilometers per year. This figure does not include the vast amounts of coal, minerals, logs, and petroleum sand carried by huge, specialized, off-road vehicles.

Winter weather provides a major challenge to Canadian roads, particularly snow and ice storms. However, Canadians have met this challenge head-on with efficient snow removal equipment and services, as well as specialized equipment for spreading sand, salt, and other melting chemicals on icy surfaces. A major winter storm that would shut down a US city for days is only a minor inconvenience in Canada, as people go about their business on quickly cleared and de-iced roads.

2. Air Transportation

Canada depends heavily on efficient air transportation services. The following table shows the number of airports in Canada:

Airports In Canada

Paved Runways	Number
Over 3333 yards	17
2666 yds to 3333 yds	15
1666 yds to 2666 yds	138
1000 yds to 1666 yds	229
Under 1000 yds	417
Total Paved	816
Unpaved Runways	
1666 yds to 2666 yds	55
1000 yds to 1666 yds	268
Total Unpaved	323

Canadian airlines carry more than 35 million passengers per year. Until mid-2000, there were two major airlines serving both domestic and international routes. These were Air Canada, which until recently was a government-owned carrier, and Canadian Airlines International, which has always been privately held. In July 2000, Canadian Airlines International Ltd. (CAI) became an indirect, wholly owned subsidiary of Air Canada, following Air Canada's purchase of a controlling interest in CAI.

In addition to these two major companies, there are close to 1000 other licensed air carriers in Canada that provide scheduled and charter services. Many Canadian communities, particularly in the North, rely solely on air services for both freight and passenger travel.

Canada has also developed a thriving aerospace industry that exports around the world. In addition to providing aircraft components, the industry provides complete aircraft for domestic service and for export to airlines throughout the world. Most notable of these are the short take-off and landing DASH-7 and DASH-8 aircraft, and the Canadair Regional Jet, all built by Bombardier, the main aerospace company of Canada. Bombardier also owns Lear Jet of the USA and Shorts Brothers of the United Kingdom, making it the third-largest aircraft manufacturer in the world.

3. Rail Transportation

Railways are a major form of freight transportation in Canada, with about 44,000 miles of standard gauge rail lines. There are two major rail companies: Canadian National Railway, which until 1995 was government owned; and Canadian Pacific Railway, which has been privately owned since its beginning in the late 1800s. The railway business is one of the largest in Canada, with annual revenues of around four billion dollars.

Railway passenger travel is handled by VIA Rail Canada, a government-owned company. VIA does not own any track, but leases it from the privately owned railways. Railway passenger travel is not popular in Canada. Only about four million passengers travel by rail each year, compared to 35 million by air.

Canada is developing highly automated light rail and subway vehicles and systems for inner-city travel. This technology and equipment is being exported around the world, particularly to Europe and the USA.

4. Marine Transportation

Canada has almost 40,000 miles of coastline, and makes extensive use of marine transportation. Annual cargo passing through Canadian ports amounts to 150 million tonnes. The main ports are Vancouver, New Westminster, and Prince Rupert on the west coast; and Halifax, Saint John, and Montreal on the east coast. The following table shows the number of various types of marine ports in Canada:

Canadian Marine Ports	
Federal ports operated by Ports Canada	14
Public ports administered by the Canadian Coast Guard	300
Private, provincial, and municipal ports	100

The St. Lawrence Seaway, a joint development with the USA, enables ocean vessels to travel deep into North America as far as Chicago. At about 2,300 miles, it is the world's longest inland waterway. It is open for about nine months each year, depending on the weather.

Canada has only a small merchant marine, relying instead on the ships of foreign registry to carry its goods. The following table lists the Canadian-owned ships of 1,000 Gross Registered Tonnage (GRT) or over.

Canadian-Owned Merchant Marine (over 1000 GRT)[1]

Oil Tanker	15
Bulk Carrier	14
General Cargo	19
Roll-on/roll-off Cargo	8
Chemical Tanker	4
Short-sea Passenger	3
Passenger	2
Railcar Carrier	2
Specialized Tanker	2
Passenger-cargo	1

Note: 1. Does not include ships used exclusively on the Great Lakes

5. Waterways and Pipelines

Canada's main inland waterway is the St. Lawrence Seaway. There are numerous smaller waterways, that are now used mainly by tourists. For example, the Rideau Canal stretches about 100 miles from Kingston, on Lake Ontario, to Ottawa, on the Ottawa River. After the War of 1812 with the USA, the British built the canal as an alternate route to the sea, to avoid the US coastline along the St. Lawrence River. It is now used mainly by American tourists.

Canada is a major petroleum producer, but unfortunately most of the wells are in western Canada, while most of the consumers are in eastern Canada. Pipelines are the main form of transportation for these products: there are 14,610 miles of crude and refined oil pipelines, and 46,488 miles of natural-gas pipelines. These stretch right across Canada and into the USA.

6. Telecommunications

On a per capita basis, Canadians are the heaviest users of telephones in the world. There are more than 15 million telephones in Canada, about one for every two people. The following table shows some of the aspects of the Canadian telephone system.

Canadian Telephone System	
Domestic satellite earth stations	300
International satellite earth stations	7
International submarine cables	5

In 1962, Canada became the third nation in space with the launch of the Alouette 1 telecommunications satellite. Since then, several follow-on and additional communications satellites have been launched to provide the Canadian telecommunications service described above. A later chapter will discuss Canada's telecommunications industry, which has business facilities throughout the world.

7. TV, Radio, and Newspapers

Canada has about 16 million television sets, or about one for every two people. There are 70 TV broadcast stations, and about 1,400 repeaters. The three major TV networks are: Canadian Television (CTV); Global TV; and the Canadian Broadcasting Corporation (CBC). As explained in chapter 3, the CBC is a government-owned network. Canadians also watch broadcasts from US stations near the border, either directly or on cable. Cable TV is very popular in Canada, as is the evolving direct satellite TV.

There are about 900 AM radio stations in Canada, and 29 FM stations. These stations, like the television stations, are controlled by the Canadian Radio and Television Corporation (CRTC), as discussed in chapter 3.

National and local newspapers in Canada are similar to those in the USA, and, in fact, some of the more prominent US newspapers (e.g., the *New York Times*) are available in Canada. American magazines are as prevalent in Canada as Canadian ones, if not more so, but

Canadian editions of US magazines are often a part of the cross-border venture, as discussed in chapter 3.

8. Additional Information

1. Government of Canada Web site: http://canada.gc.ca

10
GOVERNMENT PURCHASING

The Canadian government purchases around $14 billion (about $9 billion US) worth of goods and services each year. The Web site for Contracts Canada, <http://contractscanada.gc.ca>, contains information on how to do business with the Government of Canada, and much of the following information comes from this site. Public Works and Government Services Canada (PWGSC) is the main purchasing agency of the Canadian federal government. This chapter describes the purchasing activities of PWGSC, and how you can become a supplier. The provinces have similar purchasing arrangements, which are briefly discussed. However, your main opportunities will probably be with the federal government.

1. Trade Agreements

You should know that American companies have the right to do business with the Canadian government. Under the North American Free Trade Agreement (NAFTA), which is described in chapter 5, US companies are eligible to bid on almost all Canadian government procurements. This includes purchases made by government-owned companies called Crown Corporations. The eligible procurements include —

- government goods valued at or over $25,000
- government services valued at or over $50,000
- government construction contracts valued at or over $6.5 million
- crown corporation goods and services contracts valued at or over $250,000
- crown corporation construction contracts valued at or over $8 million

The World Trade Organization Agreement on Government Procurement (WTO-AGP) that came into effect in 1996 also allows companies from signatory countries to bid on Canadian government procurement contracts. The threshold amounts are higher than those of the NAFTA, so US companies should use the lower NAFTA limits. The WTO-AGP eligible procurements include —

- government goods and services at or over $185,000
- government construction contracts at or over $7 million

There are a number of exclusions in both the NAFTA and WTO-AGP agreements that apply to companies doing business with the government of the other country. Some of these exclusions are —

- procurements related to national security
- research and development
- health and social services
- financial and related services
- utilities
- communications, photographic, mapping, printing and publication services

- shipbuilding and ship repair
- oil purchases related to any strategic reserve requirement
- goods or services associated with safeguarding nuclear materials
- dredging work

2. What the Canadian Government Buys

The Government of Canada buys just about every kind of product and service, from aircraft to paper clips, from training services to scientific research. Public Works and Government Services Canada (PWGSC) is a common service agency responsible for a significant portion of these government requirements, which it categorizes under the following:

(a) *Architectural and Engineering Consulting Services*: Various architectural and engineering consulting services related to real property. These include —

- professional and technical services: studies, planning, design, and related services during construction for buildings, marine, air, and land facilities;

- specialized services: environmental services, electronic imaging, communication engineering, building automation, heritage restoration, and hydrographic surveys; and

- other related consulting services.

(b) *Construction and Maintenance Services*: Construction and maintenance service opportunities at or above $60,000 are advertised on MERX™. (See section on MERX below.) Opportunities below $60,000 are handled by PWGSC regional offices.

(c) *Goods and Services*: PWGSC purchases more than 17,000 types of goods and services from private sector companies on behalf of other government departments and agencies. MERX advertises requirements for most goods and services at or above $25,000. For most goods and services below this threshold, PWGSC seeks competitive bids from companies registered on PWGSC source lists. The goods and services procured include but are not limited to —

- aerospace and electronic systems (for aircraft, ships, and military vehicles);

- computer hardware and software;
- custom-manufactured and commercially available products;
- informatics services;
- marine equipment and armament;
- marine inspection and technical services;
- communications, audio-visual, and printing services;
- research and development services; and
- science and professional services.

3. Selling to the Canadian Government

There are several ways of doing business with the Canadian government. The main ones are —

- selling directly to the government departments and agencies who have authority to buy up to $5,000 worth of goods, and most services regardless of the value, directly from suppliers;
- accessing MERX, the electronic tendering service;
- adding your company to the PWGSC source lists of registered suppliers;
- becoming involved in Major Crown Projects; and
- obtaining a Standing Offer contract.

4. MERX™: The Electronic Tendering Service

MERX is an on-line service that advertises government contracting opportunities to potential bidders. MERX advertises requirements for printing services estimated at $10,000 or above, most goods and services estimated at $25,000 or above, and communications services worth $50,000 or more. Requirements estimated at $60,000 or above for realty, leasing, and maintenance services are also advertised by MERX. It also advertises requirements estimated at $72,600 or above for architectural and engineering consulting.

MERX is accessible on the Internet at <www.merx.cebra.com>, and you pay a subscription fee for additional services. At the time of writing, the fee was $7.95 Canadian per month. You can also contact the Call Centre at 1-800-964-MERX. The MERX service —

- provides the information necessary to order bid documents;

- features a menu, commands, and search terms to help you find all opportunities related to your line of business;

- provides information on what the federal government has purchased in the past, the names of the contractors, and the value of each contract;

- allows you to identify other suppliers ordering bid documents to help you determine who your competitors are, or to identify a bid partner;

- operates 24 hours a day, 7 days a week;

- offers online support; and

- provides information on other federal and provincial opportunities, as well as US and other international opportunities.

5. Government Source Lists

Source lists are used by PWGSC to solicit bids for requirements below $25,000 for many goods and services that are not advertised publicly. They are lists of companies organized by commodities and services supplied by the companies. Each entry includes the name and address of the company, and a description of the goods or services it offers. For more information on source lists and registration, contact —

Contracts Canada Information Centre
PWGSC
3C1, Place du Portage III
11 Laurier Street
Hull, Quebec K1A 0S5
Telephone: (819) 956-3440 or 1-800-811-1148
Fax: (819) 956-6123
Email: ncr.contractscanada@pwgsc.gc.ca

6. Major Crown Projects

Major Crown Projects (MCP) are procurement programs valued in excess of $100 million Canadian dollars (about $65 million US dollars). Most of these purchases are handled by the Aerospace, Marine and Electronic Systems Sector (AMES) of PWGSC. The procurement is usually done through a joint government project office, involving the specific government department that will use the goods and/or services, plus others. For example, the recently completed procurement of 12 Canadian Patrol Frigates for the Canadian Navy was done through a project office staffed by personnel from the Department of National Defence (naval and civilian), PWGSC/AEMS, and Industry Canada, whose interest was to ensure that industrial benefits were appropriately spread across Canada.

Major Crown Projects are usually lead by a Canadian prime contractor, in partnership with other major companies as major subcontractors, plus numerous additional subcontractors. The subcontractors, and sometimes the prime contractor, can come from outside the country, and there is usually considerable international involvement in these projects. For additional information, obtain the government publications *Doing Business with AMES* and *Major Crown Projects Subcontracting Opportunities*, which are available on the Internet at <http://w3.pwgsc.gc.ca/sos/text/ames/doing-e.htm>.

7. Standing Offers

Standing offers are announced and bid for in the same manner as other PWGSC contracts. They are not really contracts, however, but rather are agreements with PWGSC to provide goods or services of a defined nature, at a specified price, within a defined period of time. When a government agency requires some of these goods or services, they issue a call-up against the standing offer. Only then do you have a contract for the goods and services. The idea is to speed up procurement for relatively standard and often obtained goods and services. Standing offers are usually set up for the following:

- ♦ Food
- ♦ Fuel

- Pharmaceutical supplies
- Plumbing supplies
- Tires
- Stationary
- Electronic data processing and informatics equipment
- Repair and overhaul services
- Professional services

There are five types of standing offers:

- National Master Standing Offer (NMSO), which can be used by any government department anywhere in Canada
- Regional Master Standing Offer (RMSO), which can be used by any government department within a certain region
- National Individual Standing Offer (NISO), which can be used by a specific government department anywhere in Canada
- Regional Individual Standing Offer (RISO), which can be used by a specific government department within a certain region
- Departmental Individual Standing Offer (DISO), which can be used only by PWGSC

8. Protests

US companies having a problem with the Canadian government procurement process can contact the Commercial Section of the US Embassy in Ottawa at (613) 238-5335. There is also a formal appeal process, open to both US and Canadian companies, called the Procurement Review Board of Canada. The Board can be contacted by telephone at (613) 990-1988, or by fax at (613) 992-3686. NAFTA-related appeals are described in chapter 5.

9. Provincial Government Purchases

Provincial procurements are usually much smaller than federal requirements, and are often open only to local suppliers within the province if they can satisfy the requirement. If they cannot, the procurement is then opened to the rest of Canada, and, if required, to other countries, usually the USA. The following list has the contact information for each provincial government purchasing agency where you can obtain additional information.

Alberta
Alberta Department of Public Works
Supply and Services
6950 113th Street
Edmonton, Alberta T6H 5V7
Telephone: (403) 427-3921

British Columbia
BC Purchasing Commission
102-3350 Douglas Street
Victoria, BC V8W 9W6
Telephone: (250) 387-7300
Fax: (250) 387-7309

Manitoba
Supply and Services
Manitoba Department of Government Services
Room 101, 1700 Portage Avenue
Winnipeg, Manitoba R3J 0E1
Telephone: (204) 945-4102
Fax: (204) 948-2016

New Brunswick
New Brunswick Department of Supply and Services
P.O. Box 6000
Fredericton, New Brunswick E3B 5H1
Telephone: (506) 453-3742
Fax: (506) 444-4400

Newfoundland
Government Purchasing Agency
30 Strawberry Marsh Road
St. John's, Newfoundland A1C 4R4
Telephone: (709) 729-3348
Fax: (709) 729-5817

Nova Scotia

Nova Scotia Government Purchasing Agency
P.O. Box 787
Halifax, Nova Scotia B3J 2V2
Telephone: (902) 424-5520
Fax: (902) 424-0780

Ontario

Publications Ontario
880 Bay street, 5th Floor
Toronto, Ontario M7A 1N8
Telephone: (416) 326-5300

Prince Edward Island

Purchasing Division
Department of Finance
Shaw Building, 2nd Floor
95 Rochford Street
P.O. Box 2000
Charlottetown, PEI C1A 7N8
Telephone: (902) 386-4045

Quebec

Ministère des Approvisionnements et Services
Direction des communications
Edifice Lomer-Gouin
575, rue St-Amable
Quebec, Quebec G1R 5N9
Telephone: (418) 643-7929

Saskatchewan

Purchasing Agency
Saskatchewan Property Management Corporation
3rd Floor, 1942 Hamilton Street
Regina, Saskatchewan S4P 3V7
Telephone: (306) 787-6871
Fax: (306) 787-3023

10. Additional Information

1. Contracts Canada Information Centre, PWGSC
    3C1 Place du Portage III, Hull, Quebec K1A 0S5
    Telephone: (819) 956-3440 or 1-800-811-1148
    Fax: (819) 956-6123. Internet: contractscanada.gc.ca/

2. MERX Call Centre at 1-800-964-MERX. Web site:
    www.merx.cebra.com

3. *Doing Business with AMES* and *Major Crown Projects Sub-
    contracting Opportunities*, available from the PWGSC
    Web site:
    http://w3.pwgsc.gc.ca/sos/text/ames/doing-e.htm

4. US Embassy in Ottawa, Commercial section
    Telephone: (613) 238-5335

5. Procurement Review Board of Canada
    Telephone: (613) 990-1988. Fax: (613) 992-3686

11
MILITARY PURCHASING

Although Canada's military is small by comparison to the US forces, it is still a major purchaser of equipment and supplies. The sources of these purchases are not limited to Canada, and in fact the US is a major supplier to the Canadian military.

1. Canada's Military

The Canadian military is part of the Department of National Defence, or DND, and as such comes under the Ministery of National Defence. (In Canada 'defense' is spelled 'defence.') The Canadian military's principal defense roles, according to official government policy stated in the *1997 Canadian Defence Planning Document*, are as follows:

- ◆ Defending Canada:

    Protecting Canada's national territory and areas of jurisdiction; helping civil authorities protect and sustain national interests; ensuring an appropriate level of emergency preparedness; and assisting in national emergencies.

- ◆ Defending North America in co-operation with the United States:

    Protecting the Canadian approaches to the continent in partnership with the United States, particularly through NORAD; promoting Arctic security; and pursuing opportunities for defense cooperation with the United States in other areas.

- ◆ Contributing to International Peace and Security:

    Participating in a full range of multilateral operations through the UN, NATO, other regional organizations, and coalitions of like-minded countries; supporting humanitarian relief efforts and restoration of conflict-devastated areas; and participating in arms control and other confidence-building measures.

The Department of National Defence is divided into two parts: the military part led by the Chief of the Defence Staff (CDS), who is a general or admiral; and a mainly civilian part led by the Deputy Minister of National Defence, who is a career civil servant. Under the CDS are the Maritime Command (navy), the Land Commands (army), the Air Commands (air force), and a military personnel branch. Under the Deputy Minister are Assistant Deputy Ministers and their staff for policy, finance, infrastructure, personnel (civilian), and material. It is the Assistant Deputy Minister Material group that does almost all of the procurement for the Canadian military.

The Maritime Command, or navy, consists of approximately 9,000 regular force personnel and 4,000 primary reservists. The surface fleet consists of 16 destroyers and frigates, three operational support ships, nine countermeasures vessels, and smaller vessels for coastal patrol and training. The underwater fleet consists of three very old Oberon-class diesel submarines, which are being replace by four Upholder-class diesel submarines recently obtained from the United Kingdom. Ship-borne helicopters and long-range patrol aircraft are provided to the navy by the air force.

The Land Force Command, or army, has approximately 20,700 regular-force personnel and 18,500 reservists. They are mainly concentrated in three brigade groups that include infantry; armor; field and air defense artillery; engineers; communications; medical; military police; and combat service support. These formations have common territorial defense and domestic operations responsibilities, but each must also provide forces for peacekeeping or contingency operations abroad. The Land Forces have just received over 200 new wheeled armored reconnaissance vehicles, and is in the process of acquiring approximately 650 new armored personnel carriers.

The Air Command, or air force, has approximately 13,000 regulars and 3,000 reservists. There are four air defense squadrons, equipped with the CF-18 fighter bomber. Three maritime patrol squadrons, equipped with P-3 long-range patrol aircraft, provide support to the navy. Two maritime helicopter squadrons also provide the navy with shipborne helicopters. A strategic transport squadron is equipped with Airbus aircraft, and three tactical transport squadrons are equipped with Hercules aircraft. Two composite squadrons use a variety of aircraft for combat support, electronic-warfare training, and coastal patrol.

2. Defense Production Sharing Agreement

Since 1941 there have been a number of formal defense production agreements between the USA and Canada. The objectives of these agreements are detailed in the DOD Directive 2035.1 of November 4, 1980, part of which is shown below:

DOD Directive 2035.1 Extract

The policy of the US is to maintain and strengthen defense economic cooperation with Canada. The objectives of the policy are:

A. Promote a strong, integrated, and more widely dispersed defense industrial base in North America

B. Achieve the most economical use of research and development (R&D) and production resources

C. Foster greater standardization and interoperability of military equipment

D. Remove obstacles to the full flow of defense equipment trade

E. Encourage the exchange of information and technology

F. Accord equal consideration to the business communities of both countries

The result of these agreements and directives is that even before NAFTA, there was effectively no international border between the USA and Canada with regard to military business. Many Canadian companies are considered part of the American military-industrial complex, and, as such, are required to gear up for additional military product in times of conflict, such as during the Gulf War. The Canadian companies are allowed to bid on most US military procurement programs and requirements, and American companies are allowed to participate in Canadian military acquisition.

3. Military Procurement

Military procurement does not involve only products that are lethal. Like military forces around the world, Canada's military uses everything from major weapon systems, such as ships and submarines, to rolls of toilet paper, and they have to buy it from somebody. The major military system sales are the domain of the big companies that can afford the time and money it takes to win these contracts. Yet there is a wide range of other procurement that is open to much smaller companies, and because of NAFTA and the DPSA, American companies have an equal opportunity in this business.

The Canadian military budget is divided into two areas: operational and maintenance, and capital procurement. The table below shows the 1998–99 Department of National Defence spending estimates. (The Canadian Government fiscal year is from 1 April to 31 March of each year.)

1998—99 DND Spending Estimates
(Millions of Canadian Dollars)

	Operational & Maintenance	Capital Procurement	Total
Maritime Command	1,509	331	1,840
Land Forces Command	2,237	608	2,845
Air Command	1,912	404	2,316
Other	2,220	301	2,521
Totals	**7,878**	**1,644**	**9,522**

As with the US military, it often takes months and even years to work through the military acquisition process in Canada. You have to convince the military users and purchasing officials that your product is worthy of consideration. You then have to go through the Canadian government purchasing procedures described in chapter 10. This can take considerable effort, but hopefully, when you do eventually get the contract, it will be worth the effort. More important, you will be set up for more business with Canadian military customers.

4. Major Military Systems Procurement

From time to time the Canadian military undertakes the procurement of a major military system. For example, in the late 1980s they began the acquisition of 12 new Canadian Patrol Frigates for the navy, and in the early 1990s they let a $1.5 billion contract for the development and procurement of new communications equipment for the army. These major procurements are usually accompanied by significant political debate and acrimony, as each politician attempts to get the most for his or her voters. Regional politics and suppliers are thus very important considerations.

The usual Canadian approach to these major procurements is to have several of the larger Canadian companies band together to form consortia that bid on the projects. The consortia are almost always led by a Canadian company, but often include large foreign companies as well. For example, the consortia that won the Canadian Patrol Frigate procurement had Saint John Shipbuilding and Dry-dock Company of New Brunswick, Canada, as the prime contractor, but the combat system integrator was a company formed by Sperry Marine of the US, now part of the Lockheed Martin group. The company set up by Sperry had to locate itself in the province of Quebec in order to win the business.

The prime contractor of these major programs purchases equipment and services from many smaller companies in Canada and from around the world. The best strategy for an American company is to identify who the bidding prime contractors are, and link up with them either as a consortia member, a supplier, or a supplier to a consortia member. However, in so doing, be aware of the regional politics in Canada, and try to side with a company that offers some benefits in this regard.

5. Industrial Participation and Offsets

Canada was one of the first countries to require industrial participation and/or offsets from foreign suppliers bidding on Canadian military projects. To satisfy these requirements, the Canadian government wants a portion of the contract work done in Canada, or some other work done in Canada, as an offset against the contract. Typically, the prime contractors on large Canadian military contracts flow this requirement down to their suppliers. For example, you may be bidding on a contract to supply controllers to a US company supplying electrical generators going into Canadian navy ships. Your customer, the electrical generator manufacturer, will probably have to provide some Canadian industrial participation, and he will flow some of this requirement down to you. To be compliant in your bid, you will then have to show that you are using some Canadian components or services in association with your product. This industrial participation requirement is becoming common throughout the world.

In order to participate in Canadian military procurement programs, then, you may have to become aligned with some Canadian companies, both as customers and suppliers. There are several data bases available from Industry Canada that list Canadian companies and their products. You may also want to contact some of the relevant trade associations, some of which are described in the next section.

6. Trade Associations

There are several trade associations that are connected with doing business with the Canadian military. The most significant is the Canadian Defence Industries Association (CDIA). This started out as a branch of the American Defense Preparedness Association, which in itself shows the close ties between Canadian and American military and industry. The CDIA sponsors a number of seminars, conferences, and trade shows throughout Canada, in which US companies are welcome to participate. The association can be contacted at —

Canadian Defence Industries Association
100 Gloucester Street, Suite 202
Ottawa, ON K2P 0A4
Telephone: (613) 235-5337
Fax: (613) 235-0784

Some other trade associations dealing with the military in Canada are as follows:

- ◆ Aerospace Industries Association of Canada
- ◆ Armed Forces Communications and Electronics Association
- ◆ Canadian Shipbuilding Association

7. Additional Information

1. Canadian Department of National Defence Web site: www.dnd.ca/eng

2. *Sharing Defense Development*, US Navy International Programs Office, January 1992.

3. *United States-Canada Defense Production Sharing Program: A Question and Answer Guide for US Industry*, published by External Affairs Canada.

4. The 1997 *Canadian Defence Planning Document*, available on the Internet: www.dnd.ca/admpol/pol_docs/97defplan/table_e.htm (NOTE: more recent reports are available.)

12
RESOURCE INDUSTRIES

Canada's rich resources contribute about 7 percent to the national income. The industries associated with these resources require various imports to keep them competitive. If your product involves these resource industries, you may want to obtain more detailed information from the Government of Canada Web site, <http://canada.gc.ca>, and from the *Canada Year Book* that is annually published by Statistics Canada. This chapter covers the main points about these industries, with much of the information coming from the above-mentioned sources.

1. Oil, Gas, and Coal

Canada is the world's third largest producer of natural gas, with a production rate of over six trillion cubic feet per year. In addition to the extensive known reserves, there have been major gas discoveries in the Arctic and off the east coast. Much of this natural gas is exported to the USA via pipelines that extend down into California, the mid-west states, and the eastern seaboard.

Canada is the twelfth largest producer of crude oil, with a production rate of about two million barrels a day. (Much of this is also exported to the USA.) The remaining reserves of conventional crude oil are estimated to be more than four billion barrels. However, the Hibernia oil field, situated in the Atlantic Ocean off the coast of Newfoundland, is estimated to have considerable reserves, and the oil sands of western Canada are estimated to have the oil equivalent of the reserves of Saudi Arabia, Kuwait, and the UAE combined.

Unfortunately, most of the oil and gas production is in western Canada, and the Canadian pipelines do not extend eastward beyond Montreal. Thus, to satisfy the petroleum needs of eastern Quebec and the Atlantic provinces, Canada imports crude oil from Venezuela, Nigeria, the North Sea, and the USA. It is more economical to do this even though the country is a net exporter of energy, exporting almost entirely to the USA.

Canada is the fifth largest producer of coal in the world, providing more than 70 million tonnes per year. About half this coal is exported to countries such as Japan and South Korea. The production is mainly in western Canada, from where it is moved by specially designed trains to ocean loading facilities on the west coast. Oddly enough, Canada also imports coal from the USA for the electric generation plants in eastern Canada.

2. Electricity

Canada is the world's fifth largest producer of electricity, and is a world leader in technology and application of long-distance electrical transmission. About 60 percent of the production is from hydroelectric plants scattered throughout the country. The large hydroelectric generating complexes in James Bay and Labrador produce a huge amount of electricity that is exported to the eastern seaboard of the USA.

Canada also has 22 nuclear-powered electric generating plants, which produce close to 20 percent of the country's electrical requirements. These CANDU nuclear plants are of a unique design, and the technology has been exported to many countries around the world. Coal-fired generating plants provide much of the remaining electricity, with a small amount generated from oil and natural gas.

3. Forestry

About half of Canada is treed; the country has about 10 percent of the world's trees. As a result, Canada is the world's largest producer of newsprint, the second largest producer of pulp, and the third largest producer of lumber. Most of these forest products are exported, and in fact, Canada provides about 20 percent of the world market.

Although many think that the province of British Columbia is the main forestry producer, possibly because of the many recent environmental issues that have arisen there, it is actually Quebec that is the largest harvester of forest products. Ontario and British Columbia are next, followed by New Brunswick.

The industry is dominated by a few multinationals, based mostly in Canada but operating around the world. In some areas there is a fierce rivalry with US producers, particularly in the area of softwood lumber, which is used primarily for homebuilding. This has led to several trade disputes between the two countries.

4. Fisheries

Even though Canada is surrounded on three sides by ocean and has numerous large freshwater lakes, it is not a significant fishing nation. It ranks 15th in the world for amount of fish caught. The table below shows the quantity and value of major fish types taken in 1994, the most recent year for which information was available at the time of writing:

Major Fish Types Taken in 1994

Fish Type	Quantity (Tonnes)	Value ($000 Can)
Salmon	65,399	195,185
Herring	39,314	63,659
Clams	3,955	37,360
Halibut	5,326	33,618

Fish Type	Quantity (Tonnes)	Value ($ Can)
Crab	5,644	24,157
Shrimp	4,185	15,577
Hake	103,832	14,780
Redfish	14,903	12,588
Flatfish	6,252	4,378
Oysters	5,250	4,200

In recent years, the industry has been in rapid decline because of the dwindling stocks of cod on the east coast and salmon on the west coast. This has led to much political turmoil within the country, and to several international disputes as Canada attempts to protect the remaining fish stock against fishers from other countries.

5. Mining

Canada is the world's largest exporter of minerals, with most of the minerals produced going to the USA. Japan and Europe are the other major destinations. The following table shows the production amounts and values of the leading minerals in 1995, the most recent year for which information was available at the time of writing:

Leading Minerals in 1995		
Mineral	Production	Value (Millions $ C)
Copper	705 kilotonnes	2,684
Gold	149,027 kilograms	2,535
Nickel	167 kilotonnes	1,965
Zinc	1,094 kilotonnes	1,556
Potash	8,847 kilotonnes	1,462
Iron ore	37,130 kilotonnes	1,212
Uranium	10,094 tonnes	539

Canada is the world's leading exporter of uranium, providing more than 30 percent of the world's supply. The US alone purchases about 70 percent of the Canadian product for use in its nuclear-powered electrical generators. Japan and western Europe are also large importers of Canadian uranium.

6. Fur

The Canadian fur industry has received a lot of bad press in recent years, but in fact the industry is not very significant. In 1994, the value of ranch-raised pelts was $31 million, with mink being the predominant fur-farm animal. The value of wild pelts from trapping, mostly by aboriginal people, was only $23 million. The main wildlife species were marten, beaver, mink, and prairie wolf or coyote.

7. Trade Associations

If your business relates to Canada's resource industries, you may want to contact some of the relevant trade associations listed below.

Canadian Environmental Auditing Association
1–6820 Kitimat Road,
Mississauga, Ontario L5N 5M3
Telephone: (905) 567-4705
Fax: (905) 814-1158

Canadian Renewable Fuels Association
90 Woodlawn Road W.
Guelph, Ontario N1H 1B2
Telephone: (519) 767-0431
Fax: (519) 837-1674

Canadian Association of Mining Equipment and Services for Export
Suite 101, 345 Renfrew Drive
Markham, Ontario L3R 9S9
Telephone: 1-905-513-0046
Fax: 1-905-513-1834
Email: MINESUPPLY@CAMESE.ORG

Canadian Association of Petroleum Land Administration
440–10816 Macleod Trail S.
Calgary, Alberta T2J 5N8
Telephone: (403) 571-0640
Fax: (403) 571-0644

Canadian Association of Petroleum Producers
2100, 350–7 Avenue S.W.
Calgary, Alberta T2P 3N9
Telephone: (403) 267-1100
Fax: (403) 261-4622
Email: communication@capp.ca

Canadian Drilling Association
306–222 McIntyre Street W.
North Bay, Ontario P1B 2Y8
Telephone: (705) 476-6992
Fax: (705) 476-9494
Email: mineval@vianet.on.ca

Petroleum Communication Foundation
214, 311 Sixth Avenue S.W.
Calgary, Alberta T2P 3H2
Telephone: (403) 264-6064
Fax: (403) 237-6286

Petroleum Services Association of Canada
1150, 800–6th Avenue S.W.
Calgary, Alberta T2P 3G3
Telephone: (403) 264-4195
Fax: (403) 263-7174

Petroleum Technology Alliance Canada
8th Floor, One Palliser Square
125–9th Avenue S.E.
Calgary, Alberta T2G OP8
Telephone: (403) 268-6361
Fax: (403) 268-7520
Web site: www.ptac.org

8. Additional Information

1. Web site for Government of Canada: http://canada.gc.ca

2. *Canada Year Book*, published by Statistics Canada,
   120 Parkdale Avenue, Ottawa, ON K1A 0T6.
   Email: order@statcan.ca

13
AGRICULTURE

Canada is one of the leading food producers in the world. The agriculture industry amounts to over $82 billion each year. If your product involves this industry, you may want to obtain more detailed information at the Government of Canada Web site, <http://canada.gc.ca>, and from the *Canada Year Book*, published annually by Statistics Canada. This chapter covers only the main points about the industry, with much of the information coming from the above mentioned sources.

1. Farming Regions

Canada has four different farming regions, which have different climate and soil. These are —

♦ *Atlantic Region*: This is made up of smaller farms, growing cash crops such as fruits and vegetables. Potatoes are a significant crop.

- *Central Region*: This includes the provinces of Ontario and Quebec. It is a major corn, livestock, and dairy producing area. Other crops include maple syrup, honey, grapes (wine), and fruits. The majority of the Canadian food processing facilities are also located in this region.

- *Prairie Region*: This region is made up of the provinces of Manitoba, Saskatchewan, and Alberta. Its annual production consists of more than 50 million tonnes of wheat, oats, barley, rye, canola, and flaxseed. The harsh Canadian winter destroys most harmful crop insects and diseases, enhancing production. This region also has a large beef and dairy industry.

- *Pacific Region*: The interior of British Columbia is dominated by large cattle ranches. In the south there are flourishing fruit orchards and vineyards. Vegetables and other cash crops are grown in the coastal areas. The coastal ports are also major shipping points for prairie grain and other exported food products.

As in many other parts of the world, there is a growing trend in Canada toward larger, consolidated farms. Over 30 percent of Canadian farms now have an annual operating revenue of more than $100,000, although about half of the farms still have an income of less than $50,000 per year. The main farm incomes from various sources are shown in the table below:

Canadian Farm Income Sources in 1995

Source	Income ($million)
Cattle and calves	4,651
Dairy products	3,466
Wheat	2,791
Hogs	2,254
Canola	1,903
Other cereal and oilseed	1,730
Hens and chickens	1,051

2. Field Crops

Wheat is the major field crop in Canada, of which about 80 percent is exported. Barley is the second most important crop. Barley, oats, rye, and corn are grown mainly for livestock and poultry feed. There is a growing tendency to diversify into other crops as well, mainly canola, which produces an edible salad and cooking oil. The following table shows the field crop production figures for 1995, the most recent year for which information was available at the time of writing.

Field Crop Production in 1995	
Crop	Production (thousand tonnes)
Wheat	25,432
Barley	13,035
Corn	7,251
Canola	6,436
Oats	2,857
Soybeans	2,279
Peas	1,427
Flaxseed	1,097
Lentils	431
Rye	300

3. Livestock

Canada is a world leader in the genetic improvement of beef cattle, and Canadian cattle are known for their growth and reproductive characteristics. Dairy cattle have also been genetically improved so that the average Holstein dairy cow in Canada produces about 7700 liters of milk per year. About 85 percent of the nearly two million dairy cows in Canada are Holstein. Canadian pigs have also been developed for leanness and high quality.

The poultry industry is highly automated in Canada. A one-person operation can produce more than 12 million eggs per year. Similarly, about 640 tonnes of chicken meat can be produced by a single operator. The table below shows the livestock production in 1995.

Livestock and Livestock Products Production 1995	
Cattle and calves	14,689,000 head
Pigs	12,183,000 head
Sheep and lambs	860,000 head
Poultry	860,697 tonnes
Eggs	482,635,000 dozen
Milk and cream	7,022,000 kiloliters

4. Food Processing

Food processing in Canada is a $55 billion business. About $12 billion of this is exported, which is about 4 percent of the world market for processed food. There are more than 3000 processing plants in Canada, the majority located in Ontario and Quebec. The plants process not only the produce of Canadian farms, but also convert about $5 billion of raw food imports into processed food.

5. Trade Associations

If your business relates to Canada's agricultural industries, you may want to contact some of the relevant trade associations listed below.

Agricultural Institute of Canada
Suite 1112, 141 Laurier Avenue W.
Ottawa, Ontario K1P 5J3
Telephone: (613) 232-9459
Fax: (613) 594-5190

Canada Grains Council
Suite 330, 360 Main Street
Winnipeg, Manitoba R3C 3Z3
Telephone: (204) 942-2254
Fax: (204) 947-0992
Email: office@canadagrainscouncil.ca

Canada West Equipment Dealers Assn.
2921–15 Street N.E.
Calgary, Alberta T2E 7L8
Telephone: (403) 250-7581
Fax: (403) 291-5138

Canadian Dairy Commission
1525 Carling Avenue
Ottawa, Ontario K1A 0Z2
Telephone: (613) 792-2000
Fax: (613) 998-4492
E-mail: cdc-ccl@em.agr.ca

Canadian Egg Marketing Board
112 Kent Street, Suite 1501
Ottawa, Ontario K1P 5P2
Telephone: (613) 238-2514
Fax: (613) 238-1967
Email: info@canadaegg.ca

Canadian Farm Builders Association
P.O. Box 24021
Bullfrog Postal Outlet
Guelph, Ontario N1E 6V8
Telephone/fax: (519) 823-5634
Email: cfba@cfba.ca

Canadian Food Service Executives Association
2175 Sheppard Avenue E., Suite 310
North York, Ontario M2J 1W8
Telephone: (416) 496-0708; Toll free: 1-800-675-1189
Fax: (416) 491-1670

Canadian Forage Council
P.O. Box 4520, Station C,
Calgary, Alberta T2T 5N3
Telephone: (403) 244-4487
Fax: (403) 244-2340
Email: amc@forage.org

Canadian Pork Council
1101–75 Albert Street
Ottawa, Ontario K1P 5E7
Telephone: (613) 236-9239
Fax: (613) 236-6658

Canadian Society of Engineering in Agricultural, Food, and Biological Systems
Box 381, RPO University
Saskatoon, Saskatchewan S7N 4J8
Telephone: (306) 966-5319
Fax: (306) 966-5334
Email: csae@engr.usask.ca

Canadian Sphagnum Peat Moss Association
4 Wycliff Place
St. Albert, Alberta T8N 3Y8
Telephone: (780) 460-8280
Fax: (780) 459-0939

Canadian Wheat Board
423 Main Street
P.O. Box 816, Stn. M.
Winnipeg, Manitoba R3C 2P5
Telephone: (204) 983-0239 or 1-800-ASK-4-CWB
Fax: (204) 983-3841
Email: questions@cwb.ca

National Farmers Union
2717 Wentz Avenue
Saskatoon, Saskatchewan S7K 4B6
Telephone: (306) 652-9465
Fax: (306) 664-6226

6. Additional Information

1. Government of Canada Web site:
   http://canada.gc.ca

2. *Canada Year Book*, published by Statistics Canada, 120 Parkdale Avenue, Ottawa, ON K1A 0T6.
   Email: order@statcan.ca

14
MANUFACTURING AND CONSTRUCTION INDUSTRIES

Canada's manufacturing and construction industries account for about one-quarter of the Gross Domestic Product (GDP), and employ about one-fifth of the total Canadian workforce. If your product involves this industry, you may want to obtain more detailed information at the Government of Canada Web site, <http://canada .gc.ca>, from the *Canada Year Book*, published annually by Statistics Canada, and from the Industry Canada Web site, <www.ic .gc.ca>. This chapter covers only the main points about the industries, with much of the information coming from the above-mentioned sources.

1. Overview

As in many countries, Canada's manufacturing industries are becoming more sophisticated, leading to higher outputs but a diminishing workforce. About 75 percent of the manufacturing industries are located in Ontario and Quebec. Quebec is the major producer of textile, clothing, and paper products. Ontario has most of the other industries, led by transportation equipment, chemical products, and electrical and electronic products. The table below shows the GDP associated with most of the Canadian construction and manufacturing industries. The following sections provide basic information on those industries that would be interested in importing products.

Construction and Manufacturing Industries GDP in 1995

Industry	GDP (millions $Cdn)
Construction	27,857
Transportation equipment	15,627
Electrical and electronics	13,461
Food	10,193
Chemical and chemical products	7,857
Paper and allied products	7,855
Primary metal	7,543
Fabricated metal products	6,408
Wood industries	5,075
Printing, publishing, and allied industries	4,378
Machinery	3,765
Non-metallic mineral products	2,562
Beverage industries	2,554
Clothing industries	2,199
Plastic products	2,176
Textiles	2,000
Furniture and fixtures	1,616
Rubber products	1,589

2. Construction

As in other countries, the fortunes of the construction industry follow the economic cycles of the country. Occasional government-sponsored megaprojects add to the activity. The table below lists the value of the major segments of the Canadian construction industry. Some of these are described in the following paragraphs.

Construction Industry Value 1993

Segment	Value (millions $Cdn)
Residential building	38,433
Commercial building	11,147
Gas and oil facilities	8,081
Electric power	7,645
Road, highway, and aerodrome	6,800
Institutional building	6,205
Railway, telephone, and telegraph	3,070
Waterworks and sewage systems	3,026
Industrial building	2,594

Residential building construction is on the decline in Canada, as the population ages and the need for new housing declines. However, there is a strong trend toward spending more on housing repairs and renovations, which is keeping the industry active. Commercial building construction continues to grow as the economy grows, and there is a steady increase in institutional building construction such as convention centers and government buildings.

Infrastructure construction on roads, bridges, and sewage systems continues to increase. A recent notable example is the 27-mile-long bridge connecting mainland Canada with Prince Edward Island. The bridge rises up to 60 meters above the water to allow ocean-going vessels to pass underneath. The total cost was approximately a billion dollars.

The Canadian government is now talking about a monumental, multi-year project to upgrade the nation's roads and highways. If your products relate to this activity, you may want to keep an eye out for the start of this huge infrastructure-construction program.

3. Transportation Equipment

The transportation-equipment manufacturing category includes automobiles, trucks, busses, and railway vehicles. Automobile and truck manufacturing is inseparably tied to the US industry. This began with the Canada/USA Autopact, and continues under the North American Free Trade Agreement. Many vehicle types are built by the major auto manufacturers only in Canada for the world market. The huge parts industry that is involved is tied to other North American plants. Canadian automotive industry is the sixth largest in the world, and employs over a half-million people.

The Canadian railway equipment industry includes both the design and manufacture of equipment for railways, commuter rail service, and rapid transit such as subways. Canadian expertise in this area has been exported around the world, often in complete systems including the rails, switching, and, of course, rolling stock. Bombardier Incorporated is the main Canadian company in this area, with projects and subsidiary companies throughout the world.

4. Aerospace Industry

The Canadian aerospace industry is the fifth largest in the world. Bombardier Aerospace, part of the Bombardier Incorporated group, is the third largest aircraft manufacturer in the world. (It also owns Lear Jet of the USA and Shorts Brothers of the UK.) More than half the commercial turbine helicopters in the world are made in Canada. The industry provides the complete range of aerospace products, which are exported around the world, including —

- regional aircraft (Canadair Regional Jet, Dash 8),
- business jets (Global Express, Challenger),
- commercial helicopters,
- small and medium gas turbine engines,
- landing gear systems,
- aircraft environmental systems,
- flight simulators,

- satellite multiplexers and switches, and
- integrated space robotics systems.

If your product is intended for the aerospace industry, you may want to contact the Aerospace Industries Association of Canada for more information. They can be reached at 60 Queen Street, Suit 1200, Ottawa, ON K1P 5Y7. Telephone: (613) 232-4297; fax: (613) 232-1142; Web site: <www.aiac.ca>.

5. Electrical and Electronic

Canada's electronic industry is a world leader in innovation and production. Led by international giants such as Nortel, the products are not only sold around the world, but also manufactured in subsidiary plants throughout the world, including the USA. The major Canadian plant locations are in Toronto, Ottawa, Montreal, and Calgary. This industry is a huge consumer of component parts that are purchased from around the world. If your product involves components for the telecommunications or other electronic industry, you have a ready market in Canada.

The household appliance industry produces about one billion dollars per year. It consists of about 25 plants, mainly in the provinces of Ontario and Quebec. The major products manufactured are —

- Cooking stoves and ranges
- Refrigerators
- Dishwashers
- Freezers
- Microwave ovens
- Clothes washing machines
- Dryers
- Sewing machines

6. Chemicals

The chemical industry is Canada's fourth largest manufacturing industry, valued at around $30 billion per year. Of this total, close to half is exported, primarily to the USA. Canada is the USA's largest supplier of chemicals. On the import side, in 1995 the industry imported about $17 billion worth of products.

The industry is dominated by the large multinational companies, although there are a number of small Canadian-owned companies serving regional markets. The major products of the industry are listed below:

- Petrochemicals
- Resins
- Elastomers
- Fertilizers
- Pest Management
- Specialty chemicals
- Pharmaceuticals
- Paints and varnishes
- Soap and cleaning compounds
- Inorganic and organic chemicals

7. Clothing

The Canadian clothing industry consists mainly of small- to medium-sized companies employing less than 50 people. They produce about $7 billion worth of products per year, of which about $2 billion is exported. These exports, mainly to the USA, are predominantly men's suits.

The Canadian industry supplies only a little more than half of the Canadian requirement. In 1996 clothing imports were $3.4 billion. The primary sources were China (20 percent), the USA (19 percent), and Hong Kong (13 percent). The industry imports a wide range of fabrics as it maintains its reputation for fashion innovation and good styling.

The footwear industry also consists mainly of small- to medium-sized companies. The industry has been on the decline for several years, as Canadians become more dependent on the less expensive imports from developing countries.

8. Furniture

The Canadian household furniture industry is made up primarily of small- to medium-sized companies. They manufacture about $600 million a year, with the majority being wooden furniture. This is only about one-quarter of the Canadian requirement, so there is considerable importation of household furniture.

Office furniture is a larger industry, at about $2 billion per year. Most of the production is in Ontario. The furniture is about 60 percent metal, and the rest mainly wooden. About 55 percent of this production is exported.

9. Trade Associations

If your business relates to Canada's manufacturing industries, you may want to contact some of the relevant associations listed below.

Aerospace Industries Association of Canada
60 Queen Street, Suite 1200,
Ottawa, Ontario K1P 5Y7
Telephone: (613) 232-4297
Fax: (613) 232-1142
Web site: www.aiac.ca

Alliance of Manufacturers & Exporters Canada
5995 Avebury Road, Suite 900
Mississauga, Ontario L5R 3P9
Telephone: (905) 568-8300
Fax: (905) 568-8330

Automotive Industries Association of Canada
1272 Wellington Street
Ottawa, Ontario K1Y 3A7
Telephone: (613) 728-5821
Fax: (613) 728-6021
Email: aia@aiacanada.com
Web site: www.aiacanada.com

Automotive Parts Manufacturers Association
195 The West Mall, Suite 516
Toronto, Ontario M9C 5K1
Telephone: (416) 620-4220
Fax: (416) 620-9730
Email: info@apma.ca

Canadian Business Telecommunications Alliance
161 Bay Street, Suite 3650
PO Box 750
Toronto, Ontario M5J 2S1
Telephone: (416) 865-9993; Toll free: 1-800-668-2282
Fax: (416) 865-0859
Email: office@cbta.ca

Canadian Chemical Producers' Association
Suite 805–350 Sparks Street
Ottawa, Ontario K1R 6S8
Telephone: (613) 237-6215; Toll free: 1-800-267-6666
Fax: (613) 237-4061

Canadian Concrete Pipe Association
979 Derry Road E.
Mississauga, Ontario L5T 2J7
Telephone: (905) 565-0380; Toll free: 1-800-435-0116
Fax: (905) 565-0346
Email: info@ccpa.com

Canadian Construction Association
75 Albert Street, Suite 400
Ottawa, Ontario K1P 5E7
Telephone: (613) 236-9455
Fax: (613) 236-9526

Canadian Home Builders' Association
Email: chba@chba.ca

Canadian Institute of Plumbing and Heating
295 The West Mall, Suite 330
Etobicoke, Ontario M9C 4Z4
Telephone: (416) 695-0447
Fax: (416) 695-0450

Canadian Paint and Coatings Association
9900 Cavendish Boulevard, Suite 103
St-Laurent, Québec H4M 2V2
Telephone: (514) 745-2611
Fax: (514) 745-2031
Email: cpca@cdnpaint.org

Canadian Plastics Industry Association
5925 Airport Rd., Suite 500
Mississauga, Ontario L4V 1W1
Telephone: (905) 678-7748
Fax: (905) 678-0774

Canadian Sanitation Supply Association
300 Mill Road, #G-10
Etobicoke, Ontario M9C 4W7
Telephone: (416) 620-9320
Fax: (416) 620-9320
Email: cssa@the-wire.com

Canadian Telecommunications Consultants Association
2175 Sheppard Ave E., Suite 310
North York, Ontario M2J 1W8
Telephone: (416) 495-7761; Toll free: 1-800-463-2569
Fax: (416) 491-1670
Email: office@ctca.ca

Heating, Refrigeration & Air Conditioning Institute of Canada
5045 Orbitor Drive, Building 11, Suite 300
Mississauga, Ontario L4W 4Y4
Telephone: (905) 602-4700; Toll free: 1-800-267-2231
Fax: (905) 602-1197
Email: hraimail@hrai.ca

Japan Automobile Manufacturers Association Canada
151 Bloor Street W., Suite 460
Toronto, Ontario M5S 1S4
Telephone: (416) 968-0150
Fax: (416) 968-7095
Email: JAMA@jama.ca

Machinery and Equipment Manufacturers' Association of Canada
485 Bank Street, Suite 206
Ottawa, Ontario K2P 1Z2
Telephone: (613) 232-7213
Fax: (613) 232-7381

Royal Architectural Institute of Canada
55 Murray Street, Suite 330
Ottawa, Ontario K1N 5M3
Telephone: (613) 241-3600
Fax: (613) 241-5750
Web site: www.raic.org

10. Additional Information

1. Government of Canada Web site:
   http://canada.gc.ca

2. *Canada Year Book*, published by Statistics Canada,
   120 Parkdale Avenue, Ottawa, Ontario K1A 0T6.
   Email: order@statcan.ca

3. Industry Canada Web site:
   www.ic.gc.ca

4. *AIAC Guide 1998*, published by the Aerospace Industries
   Association of Canada, 60 Queen Street, Suite 1200
   Ottawa, Ontario K1P 5Y7
   Telephone: (613) 232-4297
   Fax: (613) 232-1142
   Web site: www.aiac.ca

15
SERVICE INDUSTRIES

As in most developed countries, the Canadian service industries are growing rapidly in comparison to other industries. In 1998 the service industries made up 73.9 percent of the Gross Domestic Product. If your product involves these industries you may want to obtain more detailed information at the Government of Canada internet site, <http://canada.gc.ca>, from the *Canada Year Book*, published annually by Statistics Canada, and from the Industry Canada Web site, <www.ic.gc.ca>.

This chapter incorporates information from the above mentioned sources to cover the main points about the industries.

1. Overview

Some of the Canadian service industries were covered in previous chapters. This chapter gives a brief outline of the major ones that were not. The table below shows the GDP associated with the major service industries in 1995.

Service Industries GDP in 1995

Industry	GDP (millions $C)
Finance and real estate	35,515
Health and social services	33,191
Educational services	28,387
Business services	25,346
Amusement and recreational services	14,244
Accommodation and food services	11,847
Personal and household services	8,574
Insurance	2,994

2. Finance and Real Estate

The Canadian banking industry is dominated by about ten large, Canadian-owned banks. The industry is fairly tightly regulated by the federal government. For example, a recent attempt by two of the largest banks to merge was blocked by the government on the grounds that it would stifle competition within Canada. Canadian banks are also very active internationally.

In addition to the banks, trust companies provide many of the banking services. In the province of Quebec, trust companies are called *caisses populaires*. Both the banks and trust companies are now developing brokerage services, either by acquiring or merging with existing brokerage companies.

The real estate industry is similar to that of the USA. It is dominated by a few large companies with branches or franchises spread across the country. Many of these companies are US based.

3. Health Services

About 10 percent of the Canadian GDP is spent on health care, which is about average for developed countries. Canada has a government-run medical system that provides medical services to all Canadians free of charge. Canadians choose their own doctors, who bill the government directly. Canadians also choose their hospitals and medically related companies, such as labs, who in turn bill the government for the services provided. If your business involves health care, you should be able to work with Canadian health care providers just as you do in the US. You should not have to get involved with the government health agencies, unless you require product certification and approval.

In spite of the government-funded healthcare system, there is still a thriving medical insurance business in Canada, which deals mainly with the out-of-country expenses of traveling Canadians. For example, the huge 'snowbird' population that travels to the southern states to avoid the Canadian winters might want additional medical coverage.

4. Business Services

There has been a huge increase in companies providing business services; many of these are self-employed individuals. The services range from the traditional accounting service, which is quite similar to that of the USA, to highly specialized consultants working as individuals or within large companies. This entire industry sector can be summed up as being very like that of the USA, and if your product is for this sector you should proceed as you would in your American market.

5. Tourism and Hospitality Industries

Tourism is an important Canadian industry and contributes over $25 billion annually to the economy. About $10 billion of this comes from foreign visitors, mainly American. (Unfortunately for Canada, Canadians spend about $15 billion a year traveling outside the country, mainly to the USA.) The main tourist attractions in Canada are the scenery, winter sports (Canada boasts several world-class skiing facilities), hunting and fishing, and shopping. The relatively low Canadian dollar provides bargains on everything from gifts to accommodation.

The range of Canadian hotels and motels is similar to that of the USA, and many of the larger chains are US based. Restaurants and fast-food outlets are also similar to those of the US, and again many are US based. If your product is for the hospitality industry, approach the people involved as you would your local customers.

6. Trade Associations

If your business relates to Canada's service industries, you may want to contact some of the relevant associations listed below.

Association of Consulting Engineers of Canada
130 Albert Street, Suite 616
Ottawa, Ontario K1P 5G4
Telephone: (613) 236-0569
Fax: (613) 236-6193

Association of Professional Computer Consultants
PO Box 24261, Hazeldean RPO
Kanata, Ontario K2M 2C3
Toll free: 1-888-ITS-APCC
Telephone: (613) 599-1948
Fax: (613) 599-1949
Email: info@apcconline.com

Canadian Business Telecommunications Alliance
161 Bay Street, Suite 3650
PO Box 705
Toronto, Ontario M5J 2S1
Toll free: 1-800-668-2282
Telephone: (416) 865-9993
Fax: (416) 865-0859
Email: office@cbta.ca

Canadian Centre for Occupational Health and Safety
250 Main Street East
Hamilton, Ontario L8N 1H6
Toll free: 1-800-668-4284
Telephone: (905) 570-8094
Fax: (905) 572-2206
Email: clientservices@ccohs.ca

Canadian Finance and Leasing Association
15 Toronto Street, Suite 301
Toronto, Ontario M5C 2E3
Telephone: (416) 860-1133
Fax: (416) 860-1140

Canadian Information Processing Society
One Yonge Street, Suite 2401
Toronto, Ontario M5E 1E5
Telephone: (416) 861-2477
Fax: (416) 368-9927
Email: astc@cips.ca

Canadian Institute of Chartered Accountants
277 Wellington Street West
Toronto, Ontario M5V 3H2
Telephone: (416) 977-3222
Fax: (416) 977-8585
Web site: www.cica.ca

Canadian Institute of Management
2175 Sheppard Avenue East, Suite 310
North York, Ontario M2J 1W8
Toll free: 1-800-387-5774
Telephone: (416) 493-0155
Fax: (416) 491-1670
Email: consult@interlog.com

Canadian Medical Association
1867 Alta Vista Drive
Ottawa, Ontario K1G 3Y6
Telephone: (613) 731-9331

Canadian Public Relations Society Inc.
220 Laurier Avenue West, Suite 720
Ottawa, Ontario K1P 5Z9
Telephone: (613) 232-1222
Fax: (613) 232-0565
Email: cprs@netcom.ca
Web site: www.cprs.ca

Canadian Real Estate Association
Email: info@crea.ca

Certified General Accountants' Association of Canada
700–1188 West Georgia Street
Vancouver, BC V6E 4A2
Telephone: (604) 669-3555
Fax: (604) 689-5845

Canadian Telecommunications Consultants Association
2175 Sheppard Ave East, Suite 310
North York, Ontario M2J 1W8
Toll Free: 1-800-463-2569
Telephone: (416) 495-7761
Fax: (416) 491-1670
Email: office@ctca.ca

Canadian Venture Capital Association
234 Eglinton Avenue East, Suite 301
Toronto, Ontario M4P 1K5
Telephone: (416) 487-0519
Fax: (416) 487-5899
Email: cvca@cvca.ca

Hotel Association of Canada
130 Albert Street, Suite 1016
Ottawa, Ontario K1P 5G4
Telephone: (613) 237-7149
Fax: (613) 238-8928

Nonprescription Drug Manufacturers Association of Canada
1111 Prince of Wales Drive, Suite 406
Ottawa, Ontario K2C 3T2
Telephone: (613) 723-0777
Fax: (613) 723-0779
Email: ndmac@ndmac.ca

Pharmaceutical Manufacturers Association of Canada
1111 Prince of Wales Drive, Suite 302
Ottawa, Ontario K2C 3T2
Telephone: (613) 727-1380
Fax: (613) 727-1407
Email: randrews@pmac-acim.org

Royal Architectural Institute of Canada
55 Murray Street, Suite 330
Ottawa, Ontario K1N 5M3
Telephone: (613) 241-3600
Fax: (613) 241-5750
Web site: www.raic.org

7. Additional Information

1. Government of Canada Web site: http://canada.gc.ca

2. *Canada Year Book*, published by Statistics Canada, 120 Parkdale Avenue, Ottawa, ON K1A 0T6. Email: order@statcan.ca

3. Industry Canada Web site: www.ic.gc.ca

16
US GOVERNMENT ASSISTANCE

The US government, mainly through the Department of Commerce (DoC), provides considerable assistance to US businesses wishing to export. This chapter outlines some of the assistance available. More detailed information can be obtained from the Web site of the DoC Commercial Service, <www.ita.doc.gov>, from where much of this information comes.

1. Department of Commerce

The job of the Commercial Service of the Department of Commerce is to help US firms to carry on international trade, particularly small- and medium-sized companies. The Commercial Service is located in more than 200 cities around the world, in about 80 countries. It provides export-related services, usually through the Export Assistance

Centers that are described in the next section. The services include the following:

- Export counseling
- Trade finance information and support
- Organization and management of trade missions and events
- Hosting and leading US government and business delegations overseas
- Market research for specific business sectors
- Credit checks on potential overseas business partners
- Identification of trade leads
- Certification of organized trade events

The Department of Commerce publishes a number of informative documents on international trade. Publications are available, for a price, from the National Technical Information Service, 5285 Port Royal Road, Springfield, VA 22161, Telephone: (703) 487-4650. Here is a list of some of the documents that pertain to Canada:

- *A Business Guide to Canada*, number PB93-177053
- *Doing Business in the Province of Quebec*, number PB91-214031
- *Economic Trends Report — Canada*, number PB93-111169
- *Guide to Packaging and Labelling Requirements in Canada*, number PB92-155548

2. Export Assistance Centers

Export Assistance Centers offer the small- and medium-size business a "one stop" shopping facility for US government export assistance. They provide the Export Assistance Programs described in the next section, and information on the programs. The Centers are located in every region of the US, including Alaska and Hawaii. Appendix B contains a listing of Center locations by state. You can find the nearest one to you by accessing their directory on the Internet at <www.ita.doc.gov/fcs/uscs/domfld.html>.

3. Export Assistance Programs

A number of export assistance programs are offered by the Department of Commerce Commercial Service. You can get details on them from the Commercial Service Web site at <www.ita.doc.gov/uscs /uscshelp.html>. Some of the programs that apply to exporting to Canada include—

- *National Trade Data Bank* (*NTDB*): A collection of about 200,000 documents, including market research reports on various countries. A considerable amount of information on Canada is available.

- *Economic Bulletin Board* (*EBB*): Up-to-date information of trade leads, market statistics, etc. You have to subscribe to the service.

- *Industry Sector Analysis*: Market research reports on various overseas markets. These are available on the NTDB and EBB.

- *International Market Insights*: Short profiles of specific market conditions or opportunities. These are available on the NTDB and EBB.

- *Customized Market Analysis*: Report assessing the specific foreign market for your specific product.

- *Trade Opportunity Program*: Sales leads from international firms looking for US products. They are available on the EBB.

- *Agent/Distributor Service*: Customized search in a specific country for qualified agents and/or distributors for your product.

- *International Company Profile*: Information on potential trading partners.

- *Country Directory of International Contacts*: Names and relevant information concerning potential importers and agents in specific countries.

4. US Embassy and Consulates in Canada

You can also get assistance from the US embassy in Ottawa, and the US consulates across Canada. View the addresses and telephone numbers listed below to determine which embassy is most convenient for you:

The United States Embassy
490 Sussex Drive
Ottawa, Ontario K1N 1G8
Telephone: (613) 238-5335

US **Consulate General**
Suite 1050, 615 Macleod Trail, S.E.
Calgary, Alberta T2G 4T8
Telephone: (403) 265-8962

US **Consulate General**
Suite 910, Cogswell Tower, Scotia Square
Halifax, Nova Scotia B3J 3K1
Telephone: (902) 429-2480

US **Consulate General**
P.O. Box 65, Postal Station Desjardins
Montreal, Quebec H5B 1G1
Telephone: (514) 398-9695

US **Consulate General**
2 Place Terrasse, C.P. 939
Quebec City, Quebec G1R 4T9
Telephone: (418) 692-2095

US **Consulate General**
360 University Avenue
Toronto, Ontario M5G 1S4
Telephone: (416) 595-1700

US **Consulate General**
1095 West Pender Street
Vancouver, British Columbia V6E 2M6
Telephone: (604) 685-4311

5. Canadian Embassy and Consulates in the USA

Although the Canadian embassy and consulates in the USA are more interested in helping Canadian companies do business in the US, you might want to contact them for information on Canada. Their addresses and telephone numbers are listed below:

Embassy of Canada
501 Pennsylvania Avenue N.W.
Washington, D.C. 20001
Telephone: (202) 682-1740

Canadian Consulate General
1175 Peachtree Street N.E.
100 Colony Square, Suite 1700
Atlanta, GA 30361
Telephone: (404) 532-2000

Canadian Consulate General
Three Copley Place, Suite 400
Boston, MA 02116
Telephone: (617) 262-3760

Canadian Consulate General
One Marine Midland Center, Suite 3000
Buffalo, NY 14203-2884
Telephone: (716) 858-9500

Canadian Consulate General
Two Prudential Plaza
Suite 2400, 180 N. Stetson Avenue
Chicago, IL 60601
Telephone: (312) 616-1860

Canadian Consulate General
St. Paul Tower, Suite 1700
750 North St. Paul Street
Dallas, TX 75201
Telephone: (214) 922-9806

Canadian Consulate General
600 Renaissance Center, Suite 1100
Detroit, MI 48243-1798
Telephone: (313) 567-2340

Canadian Consulate General
550 S. Hope Street, 9th Floor
Los Angeles, CA 90071
Telephone: (213) 346-2756

Canadian Consulate General
701 4th Avenue South, Suite 900
Minneapolis, MN 55415-1899
Telephone: (612) 332-7486

Canadian Consulate General
1251 Avenue of the Americas
New York, NY 10020-1175
Telephone: (212) 596-1659

Canadian Consulate General
412 Plaza 600, Sixth and Stewart Streets
Seattle, WA 98101-1286
Telephone: (206) 443-1777

6. Additional Information

1. Department of Commerce Commercial Service Web site: <www.ita.doc.gov>.

2. *A Business Guide to Canada*, publication number PB93-177053, published by the National Technical Information Service, 5285 Port Royal Road, Springfield, VA 22161, Telephone: (703) 487-4650.

3. *Doing Business in the Province of Quebec*, publication number PB91-214031, published by the National Technical Information Service, 5285 Port Royal Road, Springfield, VA 22161, Telephone: (703) 605-6000.

4. *Economic Trends Report — Canada*, publication number PB93-111169, published by the National Technical Information Service, 5285 Port Royal Road, Springfield, VA 22161, Telephone: (703) 605-6000.

5. *Guide to Packaging and Labelling Requirements in Canada*, publication number PB92-155548, published by the National Technical Information Service, 5285 Port Royal Road, Springfield, VA 22161, Telephone: (703) 605-6000.

6. Export Assistance Center directory Web site: <www.ita.doc.gov/fcs/uscs/domfld.html>

17
PROMOTING YOUR PRODUCT

Promoting your product in Canada will not be much different from the way you promote it in the US. There are some differences, mainly in the province of Quebec, but your usual approach should generally work. This chapter explains some of the adjustments that you may have to make.

1. Brochures

As you no doubt know, you must have some kind of brochure to tell customers about your product. Initially, you can use the same brochure you use in the USA. However, if your product is heavily dependent on measurements, you will eventually have to convert it into metric equivalents. There is no need to worry about it initially, though, as Canadians still relate to the old system of feet and pounds.

If your main business will be in the province of Quebec, you may have to have your brochure translated into French. Besides the translation itself, there is another problem associated with changing a brochure from English to French. French takes about 20 percent more space to say the same thing, and it may not fit into your current layout. You may have to juggle the artwork accordingly.

On the topic of artwork, there is a trick you can use to reduce your brochure costs when translating it into other languages. When you are producing a new brochure, and are not yet prepared to have it translated into a foreign language, you may want to allow for a future translation. The most expensive part of printing a brochure is doing the colored pictures and artwork. In the production process, the colored work is usually printed first, and the words, usually in black, are then printed onto the colored work. So when you print the brochures, have the printer print extra copies with just the colored work printed on them. Then, when you decide to print the brochure in another language, you just have to print the translated words onto the colored work — if they fit, of course.

2. Other Marketing Material

Videotapes explaining products are as popular in Canada as they are in the US. You may not know that there is a problem with videotapes in different parts of the world. Tapes used in North America will not work on European machines, and vice versa. In North America the standard electronic format videotape is called NTSC, and in Europe the format is called PAL. France and Russia use another system (SECAM), and Japan uses a different version of NTSC. You will be happy to know that Canada uses the same system (NTSC) as the USA does. You will not have to change your current tape, unless you want to have a French version.

Gifts are not a big deal in Canada, as they are in some other countries, but small gifts with company logos are a useful addition to your marketing. As you know, there are many such items available now, ranging from cheap and useless to distinctive and expensive. Try to select something uniquely tied to your product. Also bear in mind the status of the customer who will receive the gift. A CEO of a large company will not be impressed with a plastic key chain.

3. Advertising

Advertising in Canada is much the same as in the USA. For example, many of the TV ads for products sold in both countries are the same. But there are some subtle differences. Canadians do not respond well to the heavy-handed, "in-your-face" ads used by some companies. They tend to be more appreciative of witty or sophisticated ads. If you do decide to advertise on TV (or radio), you should do so through a Canadian ad agency to ensure that you get the tone right. You might also want to watch a few Canadian TV ads to see the difference.

Although most of the major US magazines are also sold in Canada, many of them change the ads to target the Canadian audience. So don't assume that your ad placed in a US magazine will also appear in Canada in the same magazine. If you want to use magazine ads, once again, you should work through a Canadian ad agency to ensure that you get the right slant, and the right magazine.

You should also consider having articles about your product published in relevant magazines or newspapers. Quite often, if you provide the editor with a written article and suitable artwork, he or she will publish the article. The magazine will probably hound you to buy some advertising space, which you may also want to do to complement your article. This can be a very cost-effective way of advertising.

4. Trade Shows

Trade shows are an excellent way of promoting your products, testing the response to your product in a new market, and identifying potential Canadian distributors or business partners. However, as in the US, trade shows have become a product in themselves, and as such there are too many for the potential customers to attend. So before you choose a trade show, carefully consider it. Make sure that the customer audience you want to target will be in attendance in numbers that will make your efforts worthwhile.

Once you have decided to use a trade show to promote your product in Canada, there are a number of issues that you must resolve in order to ensure a successful show. Some of these are different from the issues you encounter in the US, so they are reviewed below with a Canadian slant:

Booth Size and Type: Your booth size in Canada should be a multiple of the standard 9-square-meter booth, about 10 feet by 10 feet.

Exhibit: You must ensure that you exhibit the products for a Canadian audience. You will be happy to know that your demonstration equipment will work just as well in Canada as in the USA. (But don't count on this in other countries.)

Artwork: You will need some artwork in the booth to help display your product. If the trade show is in the province of Quebec, you will have to have at least some of it in French.

Press Kits: You should prepare a number of press kits to give out to press people when they come looking for material to write about. Even if they do not come around, find them and give them a kit. The kit should have a brief magazine-style article about your product. You should also include 8" by 10" glossy pictures of your product that the press can publish with your article. You can include your brochures, but the press people will be more interested in the article and the pictures.

5. Temporary Importing/Exporting of Goods for Exhibiting

To take demonstration equipment into a foreign country for trade shows, demonstrations to prospective customers, or to give the equipment to a prospective customer to try it out for a short period of time, you must become involved with temporary importing and exporting. In effect, the equipment is exported from your country, imported into the foreign country, then exported from the foreign country, and imported back into your country. This activity could incur import duties in both the foreign country and your own. Most countries recognize this problem and have taken steps to avoid these duty costs.

The most common way of temporarily moving equipment across international borders is by an internationally recognized document called a carnet (pronounced "car-nay"). It was developed by the International Bureau of Chambers of Commerce, and it allows you to export goods temporarily into another country and re-export them back to your own country without going through extensive customs procedures or paying duties.

However, the North American Free Trade Agreement makes it even easier to bring equipment into Canada. There are some simple forms to fill out at the US Customs office as you cross the border, which you must also show on your return. It is merely a matter of minimal paperwork, but you must go through the procedure. After all, you are importing and exporting across an international border.

6. Local Briefings and Seminars

During your visits to Canada you will have to brief potential customers, either as an introduction to your product or to reinforce previous exposure. These briefings will almost always be in English, although some customers in Quebec may insist on a French briefing. You will then have to work through an interpreter. However, bear in mind that they will probably understand English even though they will not always understand all that you are saying.

Seminars on your product are also a very useful marketing tool, provided, of course, that the product lends itself to this type of promotion. The seminar can be as short as a few hours or as long as a few days. The usual procedure is for you or your agent/distributor to send out invitations to potential customers to attend the seminar at an announced time and place. The agent usually selects the people and organizations that will be invited, and he or she also sends out the invitations, usually by fax. Keep in touch with the agent when he or she is making these arrangements to make sure that all the facts are right, including the dates when you will be available. You then give a detailed briefing on the product to the assembled customers. The briefings can be as elaborate as you want to make them. The main thing to remember is that the people attending are probably genuinely interested in a product of your type.

7. Follow-up

Every marketing and sales course stresses the need for follow-up. This is even more important in international marketing, wherein the term "out of sight, out of mind" is particularly true. The best follow-up is to keep regularly in touch with your potential customers or your agent/distributor. Send them new brochures and new product information as they become available. Telephone or fax them about once a week, either for an update on the business opportunity, or just to talk. The main thing to remember is to keep following up. If you don't, all of your initial effort will be wasted.

8. Additional Information

1. *Developing International Markets*, by Gerhard W. Kautz. Published by The Oasis Press/PSI Research, Grants Pass, Oregon, 1998.

18
BUSINESS TRIPS TO CANADA

A business trip to Canada is not much different from one to your neighboring state. Yet you are going into another country, and you will have to contend with Customs and Immigration issues. There are some subtle differences that you will encounter during your business visits. This chapter covers these issues and differences. For additional information, see the Canadian Department of Foreign Affairs and International Trade Web site page on business trips to Canada at <www.investincanada.ic.gc.ca>, from where much of this information was obtained.

1. Entrance Requirements

Because of the special relationship between Canada and the USA, US citizens and permanent residents of the USA do not require a passport to enter Canada. They must have some form of identification, such as a birth certificate, that shows them to be citizens or residents of the USA. (Citizens of other countries require a passport, and some also require a visa to visit Canada.)

Business visitors covered under the North American Free Trade Agreement (NAFTA) do not require work authorization, regardless of the length of stay. They must have proof of US or Mexican citizenship, meet the general requirements pertaining to health and security, and qualify as one of the following: business visitor, intra-company transferee, trader or investor, or professional. These categories are described in chapter 5, and the list of NAFTA qualifying professions is provided in Appendix A.

You will of course have to pass through Canadian Customs and Immigration checks at the border or arrival airport. You will be permitted to bring personal goods into Canada for your own use, provided that they will be taken back out of Canada when you leave. Gifts may be brought in duty and tax free, provided they do not exceed $60 in value and are not alcohol or tobacco. Animals, food, and plants brought into Canada are subject to special regulations. For more information on the import regulations, contact —

Revenue Canada Customs
Customs Building, 1st Floor
2265 St. Laurent Boulevard
Ottawa, Ontario K1G 4K3
Telephone: (613) 991-0501
Fax: (613) 991-1407

2. Travel Considerations

Remember that Canada has two official languages: English and French. English is the business language throughout most of Canada, including most of Quebec. However, in Quebec you may run across situations in which people do not understand English. Also, be forewarned that all highway signs in Quebec are in French only, but this is not usually a problem.

The airports in the major Canadian cities are like those in the USA, with all the usual facilities such as car-rental agencies, taxis, and busses to downtown hotels. The international airports (most of the airports are international) also have currency exchanges where you can get Canadian money. Canada's road system is on a par with that of the USA. And, in case you are wondering, Canadians do drive on the right-hand side, just like Americans.

The range of available hotels is also similar to that of the USA. Most offer the usual business services, and suites hotels are becoming quite popular. Restaurants are as prolific in Canada as in the US, with many ethnic varieties available. If you need a fast-food fix, you will be happy to know that most of the major US chains are also in Canada.

Even though Canada has universal health coverage free of charge, it is free to only Canadian citizens. You will be able to access it without any problem, but you will have to pay. Make sure that your health insurance covers you outside of the USA, and if it does not, you will need to take out some travel medical insurance.

3. Currency, Credit Cards, and Banks

The Canadian dollar comes in paper denominations of 5, 10, 20, 50, 100, 500, and 1000. There is a one-dollar coin commonly referred to as a 'loony' because it has a picture of a loon on it. A recent addition is a two-dollar coin that is commonly referred to as a 'twoony' after the loony. Other coins are in denominations of 1, 5, 10, and 25 cents. The symbol for the dollar is the same as in the US ($), and also the same for the cents (¢). Dollars and cents, when written, are separated by a decimal point as in the US (for example, $19.95). However, there is a growing trend in Quebec toward the French method of using a comma to separate dollars and cents (such as $19,95).

You will be pleasantly surprised to get about one-and-a-half as many Canadian dollars for the American dollars you exchange. At the time of writing, the Canadian dollar was at about $0.65 US. You will be even more pleasantly surprised to see that most listed prices are the same as in the USA, but in Canadian dollars; you will be saving about a third of the cost. Needless to say, US visitors to Canada enjoy shopping!

All of the major US credit cards are honored in Canada, although many businesses limit them to Visa, Mastercard, and perhaps American Express. When you use your credit card in Canada, the amount will be in Canadian dollars. When you receive your bill back home, the credit card company will have converted the amount to US dollars.

Banks and Automated Teller Machines (ATMs) are as prolific in Canada as in the US. Many ATMs will also allow you to access your own bank back home, for a small service fee. The major traveler's checks are accepted by almost all businesses. By the way, in Canada the word 'check,' as in negotiable instrument, is spelled 'cheque,' but the word is pronounced the same as in the US.

4. Local Business Practices

Local business practices in Canada are similar to those of the US. Appointments are arranged in advance for a specific date and time, and are usually kept. (This is not always the situation in other countries.) In general, Canadians like to be prompt for their appointments, and expect others to be as well. If you are going to be late, or have to cancel, a telephone call to the person you are meeting will be appreciated and usually understood.

Business hours for most companies are from 8:00 a.m. to 5:00 p.m., Monday through Friday. Very few businesses are open on the weekend, with the exception of retail stores. Government offices are usually open from 8:30 a.m. to 4:30 p.m., Monday through Friday. Most banks are open from 10:00 a.m. to 3:00 p.m. Monday through Friday, but some have longer hours and are open on Saturday as well. ATMs are always open.

Just like in the USA, all of Canada, except Saskatchewan, observes daylight saving time. The clocks are advanced an hour the first Sunday in April, and turned back an hour on the last Sunday in October. The time zones in Canada are shown in the following table:

Canadian Time Zones

Province	Time Zone	Compared to New York
Newfoundland	Newfoundland Standard Time	1½ hours ahead of New York
Nova Scotia New Brunswick Prince Edward Island	Atlantic Standard Time	1 hour ahead of New York

Province	Time Zone	Compared to New York
Quebec Ontario	Eastern Standard Time	Same as New York
Manitoba Saskatchewan	Central Standard Time	1 hour later than New York
Alberta	Mountain Standard Time	2 hours later than New York
British Columbia	Pacific Standard Time	3 hours later than New York

Holidays in Canada are slightly different to those in the USA. The following table lists the holidays that are usually observed by government offices and most businesses.

National Holidays in Canada

Holiday	Date
New Year's Day	January 1
Good Friday	Friday before Easter Sunday
Easter Monday	Monday after Easter Sunday
Victoria Day	Monday on or before May 24
Canada Day	July 1
Labour Day	First Monday in September
Thanksgiving Day	Second Monday in October
Remembrance Day	November 11
Christmas Day	December 25
Boxing Day	December 26

5. Goods and Services Tax (GST)

If you have traveled in Europe, you will probably have run across the Value Added Tax or VAT. Well, Canada has a similar tax called the Goods and Services Tax, or GST. This is a federal tax of 7 percent, imposed on many goods and almost all services across the country. It is in addition to the Provincial Sales Tax (PST), which ranges from 0 to 12 percent, and is imposed by the provinces on most items. In the Atlantic provinces the GST and PST have been combined to form the Harmonized Sales Tax (HST) of 15 percent.

The good news is that you can get a refund for the GST paid on short-term accommodation (less than one month) and certain goods, if you meet the following criteria:

♦ You are not a resident of Canada

♦ You paid tax on the goods and/or accommodation

♦ You bought the goods for use outside of Canada

♦ You removed the goods from Canada within 60 days

♦ You have original receipts

♦ Your receipts each show a minimum purchase amount, before taxes, of $50 Canadian

♦ Your total purchase amounts to at least $200 Canadian.

To claim the refund, you have to complete the Revenue Canada form "Visitor Application for Refund of Goods and Services Tax/Harmonized Sales Tax." The form, together with your original receipts, some identification and proof of export, can be given to most duty free shops at the border (not at an airport). You can also mail it to Revenue Canada when you get home. For more information on the GST refund, and for a copy of the application form, obtain a copy of the pamphlet "Tax Refund For Visitors" from any Canadian Customs office as you enter or leave Canada.

6. General Considerations

Clothing worn in Canada is similar to that of most of the USA. The climate in Canada is not much worse than that of the northern US states. (See chapter 2 for typical temperatures.) Don't arrive in Toronto in July in an overcoat, because in all likelihood the temperature and humidity will be in the nineties. Of course you will not want to visit Ottawa or Edmonton in January without an overcoat. The temperatures there can dip to -30° or -40° Celsius (the Celsius and Fahrenheit scales meet at about -40°).

Electric current is the same as that in the USA. That is, 110 volts and 60 cycles. Wall plugs are also similar. As mentioned in a previous chapter, the TV transmission and VCR recording format is similar to that of the USA. All of these are usually different outside of North America.

Tipping in Canada is the same as in the USA. Some restaurants add a tip or service charge onto the bill, so make sure that you do not tip twice. In general, the tip is 10 to 15 percent of the charge.

Shopping in Canada is a treat for foreign visitors because of the low Canadian dollar. Many standard items are priced as they would be in the US, except in Canadian dollars rather than US dollars — that is, about a third less. You will, however, be surprised at the high cost of cigarettes and liquor. Most of the cost is due to federal and provincial taxes that, on these items, are referred to as 'sin tax.' Consequently, most Canadians do not object to this form of taxation.

7. Additional Information

1. Canadian Department of Foreign Affairs and International Trade page on business trips to Canada Web site: www.investincanada.ic.gc.ca

2. For information on import regulations contact:
   Revenue Canada Customs, Customs Building, 1st Floor, 2265 St. Laurent Boulevard, Ottawa, Ontario K1G 4K3.
   Telephone: (613) 991-0501 Fax: (613) 991-1407

3. *Tax Refund For Visitors* pamphlet, obtainable from any Canadian Customs office.

19
SHIPPING INTO CANADA

Even before you have made a sale in Canada, you may have to ship samples or demonstration equipment into the country. This chapter covers some of the basic issues you will have to face in order to get your goods across the border. Some of the information in this chapter comes from the Revenue Canada pamphlet entitled *Guide to Importing Commercial Goods*, which you may want to consult for additional information.

1. Customs Broker

Customs brokers are commercial companies who help importers get through the complex process of bringing goods into a country. In Canada they are licensed by Revenue Canada to carry out customs-related responsibilities on behalf of their clients. (The Canadian

Customs Service comes under the Canadian federal government department called Revenue Canada.) Customs brokers charge a fee for their services, which include —

- advising you on tariff classifications, duty rates, fees, rules of origin, and other pertinent issues;
- obtaining, preparing, and presenting or transmitting the necessary documents or data;
- paying any duties that apply on your behalf;
- obtaining release of the imported goods;
- maintaining records; and
- responding to any Revenue Canada concerns after payment.

It is highly recommended that you use a Customs broker, at least for your initial shipments into Canada. The documentation and bureaucracy is far too complex for you to deal with comfortably, particularly if you are at a distance from the Canadian Customs office. Probably the easiest way for you to get a customs broker is to have your Canadian business contact recommend one. If necessary, he or she can find one in the *Yellow Pages* of the Canadian city to which you are shipping.

2. Documentation Required

The documentation required to ship imports into Canada is listed below, and explained in the following paragraphs:

- Invoice
- Cargo Control Document (CCD)
- Canada Customs Coding Form, Form B3
- Certificate of Origin
- Required import permits, health certificates, or other special documentation, as applicable

Canada Customs prefers that you use their Canada Customs Invoice (CCI), a copy of which is shown on the following page. However, you can use any commercial invoice that indicates the buyer, seller, country of origin, price paid or payable, quantity of the goods, and a detailed description of the goods.

Sample 2
Canadian Customs Invoice

■✦■ Canada Customs and Revenue Agency	Agence des douanes et du revenu du Canada	**CANADA CUSTOMS INVOICE** **FACTURE DES DOUANES CANADIENNES**	Page of de

1. Vendor (name and address) - Vendeur (nom et adresse)	2. Date of direct shipment to Canada - Date d'expédition directe vers le Canada
	3. Other references (include purchaser's order No.) Autres références (inclure le n° de commande de l'acheteur)

4. Consignee (name and address) - Destinataire (nom et adresse)	5. Purchaser's name and address (if other than consignee) Nom et adresse de l'acheteur (s'il diffère du destinataire)
	6. Country of transhipment - Pays de transbordement
	7. Country of origin of goods Pays d'origine des marchandises / IF SHIPMENT INCLUDES GOODS OF DIFFERENT ORIGINS ENTER ORIGINS AGAINST ITEMS IN 12. SI L'EXPÉDITION COMPREND DES MARCHANDISES D'ORIGINES DIFFÉRENTES, PRÉCISEZ LEUR PROVENANCE EN 12.

8. Transportation: Give mode and place of direct shipment to Canada Transport : Précisez mode et point d'expédition directe vers le Canada	9. Conditions of sale and terms of payment (i.e. sale, consignment shipment, leased goods, etc.) Conditions de vente et modalités de paiement (p. ex. vente, expédition en consignation, location de marchandises, etc.)
	10. Currency of settlement - Devises du paiement

11. Number of packages Nombre de colis	12. Specification of commodities (kind of packages, marks and numbers, general description and characteristics, i.e., grade, quality) Désignation des articles (nature des colis, marques et numéros, description générale et caractéristiques, p. ex. classe, qualité)	13. Quantity (state unit) Quantité (précisez l'unité)	Selling price - Prix de vente	
			14. Unit price Prix unitaire	15. Total

18. If any of fields 1 to 17 are included on an attached commercial invoice, check this box Si tout renseignement relativement aux zones 1 à 17 figure sur une ou des factures commerciales ci-attachées, cochez cette case Commercial Invoice No. / N° de la facture commerciale ☐	16. Total weight - Poids total Net / Gross - Brut	17. Invoice total Total de la facture

19. Exporter's name and address (if other than vendor) Nom et adresse de l'exportateur (s'il diffère du vendeur)	20. Originator (name and address) - Expéditeur d'origine (nom et adresse)

21. CCRA ruling (if applicable) - Décision de l'Agence (s'il y a lieu)	22. If fields 23 to 25 are not applicable, check this box Si les zones 23 à 25 sont sans objet, cochez cette case ☐

23. If included in field 17 indicate amount: Si compris dans le total à la zone 17, précisez :	24. If not included in field 17 indicate amount: Si non compris dans le total à la zone 17, précisez :	25. Check (if applicable): Cochez (s'il y a lieu) :
(i) Transportation charges, expenses and insurance from the place of direct shipment to Canada Les frais de transport, dépenses et assurances à partir du point d'expédition directe vers le Canada	(i) Transportation charges, expenses and insurance to the place of direct shipment to Canada Les frais de transport, dépenses et assurances jusqu'au point d'expédition directe vers le Canada	(i) Royalty payments or subsequent proceeds are paid or payable by the purchaser Des redevances ou produits ont été ou seront versés par l'acheteur ☐
(ii) Costs for construction, erection and assembly incurred after importation into Canada Les coûts de construction, d'érection et d'assemblage après importation au Canada	(ii) Amounts for commissions other than buying commissions Les commissions autres que celles versées pour l'achat	(ii) The purchaser has supplied goods or services for use in the production of these goods L'acheteur a fourni des marchandises ou des services pour la production de ces marchandises ☐
(iii) Export packing Le coût de l'emballage d'exportation	(iii) Export packing Le coût de l'emballage d'exportation	☐

Dans ce formulaire, toutes les expressions désignant des personnes visent à la fois les hommes et les femmes.

CI1 (00) Printed in Canada - Imprimé au Canada A466   A466

The Cargo Control Document (CCD) is used to report the shipment to Canada Customs, and a copy is also sent to you to inform you that your shipment has arrived. If your goods must be put in a bonded or sufferance warehouse, the CCD is also the controlling document for this activity. Many carriers have their own CCD form, however, Canada Customs prefers the use of their own Form A8A, Customs Cargo Control Document.

Form B3, Canada Customs Coding Form, is the form on which the duties and taxes are listed. A copy of this form is included, and is also available on the Internet at <www.ccra_adrc.gc.ca/E/pbg/cf /b3bq/README.html>. Correct completion of Form B3 is very important, and it is recommended that you have a Customs broker assist you in this. The information on the form should include —

♦ name of the importer and the import/export account;

♦ description of the goods;

♦ direct shipment date;

♦ tariff treatment;

♦ country of origin;

♦ tariff classification;

♦ value for duty;

♦ appropriate duty or tax rates; and

♦ calculation of duties owing.

The Certificate of Origin (see Sample 1) determines the tariff treatment your goods will receive. There are different duty rates for different goods, and more important, for different countries and trade agreements that Canada has with those countries. For example, under NAFTA you will receive the best tariff treatment and lowest duty rates, if any at all, but the Certificate of Origin must prove this eligibility. Certificates of Origin are covered in more detail in chapter 5.

Additional import permits, health certificates, or other documentation may be required, depending on the goods. For example, you will require a certificate of examination for meat products. Import permits will be required for controlled and restricted drugs. If your product is in this area, you are strongly advised to seek the help of a customs broker, at least for your first import into Canada.

Sample 3
Form B3, Canada Customs Coding Form

Canada Customs and Revenue Agency — Agence des douanes et du revenu du Canada

CANADA CUSTOMS CODING FORM
DOUANES CANADA - FORMULE DE CODAGE

PROTECTED (WHEN COMPLETED)
PROTÉGÉ (UNE FOIS REMPLI)

1 IMPORTER NAME AND ADDRESS / NOM ET ADRESSE DE L'IMPORTATEUR — NO. - N°

2 TRANSACTION NO. - N° DE TRANSACTION

3 TYPE | 4 OFFICE NO. N° DE BUREAU | 5 GST REGISTRATION NO. N° DE TPS | 6 PAYMENT CODE CODE DE PAIEMENT | 7 MODE OF TRANS. MODE DE TRANS. | 8 PORT OF UNLADING PORT DE DÉBARQ. | 9 TOTAL VFD - TOTAL DE LA VD

10 SUB HDR NO. N° DE SOUS-EN-TÊTE | 11 VENDOR NAME - NOM DU VENDEUR — NO. - N°

12 COUNTRY OF ORIGIN PAYS D'ORIGINE | 13 PLACE OF EXPORT LIEU D'EXPORTATION | 14 TARIFF TREATMENT TRAITEMENT TARIFAIRE | 15 U.S. PORT OF EXIT BUREAU DE SORTIE DES É.-U.

16 DIRECT SHIPMENT DATE DATE D'EXPÉDITION DIRECTE (Y/A M D/J) | 17 CRCY. CODE CODE DEVISE | 18 TIME LIMIT - DÉLAI | 19 FREIGHT - FRET

20 RELEASE DATE - DATE DE LA MAINLEVÉE

RESERVED FOR CCRA USE
RÉSERVÉ À L'USAGE DE L'AGENCE

21 LINE LIGNE | 22 DESCRIPTION DÉSIGNATION | 23 WEIGHT IN KILOGRAMS POIDS EN KILOGRAMMES | PREVIOUS TRANSACTION - TRANSACTION ANTÉRIEURE: 24 NUMBER NUMÉRO, 25 LINE LIGNE | 26 SPECIAL AUTHORITY AUTORISATION SPÉCIALE
27 CLASSIFICATION NO. N° DE CLASSEMENT | 28 TARIFF CODE TARIFAIRE | 29 QUANTITY QUANTITÉ | 30 U - M | 31 VFD CODE CODE VD | 32 SIMA CODE CODE DE LMSI | 33 RATE OF CUSTOMS DUTY TAUX DE DROIT DE DOUANE | 34 E.T. RATE TAUX T.A. | 35 RATE OF GST TAUX DE TPS | 36 VALUE FOR CURRENCY CONVERSION CONVERSION VALEUR POUR CHANGE
37 VALUE FOR DUTY VALEUR EN DOUANE | 38 CUSTOMS DUTIES DROITS DE DOUANE | 39 SIMA ASSESSMENT COTISATION DE LMSI | 40 EXCISE TAX TAXE D'ACCISE | 41 VALUE FOR TAX VALEUR POUR TAXE | 42 GST TPS

21 LINE LIGNE | 22 DESCRIPTION DÉSIGNATION | 23 WEIGHT IN KILOGRAMS POIDS EN KILOGRAMMES | PREVIOUS TRANSACTION - TRANSACTION ANTÉRIEURE: 24 NUMBER NUMÉRO, 25 LINE LIGNE | 26 SPECIAL AUTHORITY AUTORISATION SPÉCIALE
27 CLASSIFICATION NO. N° DE CLASSEMENT | 28 TARIFF CODE TARIFAIRE | 29 QUANTITY QUANTITÉ | 30 U - M | 31 VFD CODE CODE VD | 32 SIMA CODE CODE DE LMSI | 33 RATE OF CUSTOMS DUTY TAUX DE DROIT DE DOUANE | 34 E.T. RATE TAUX T.A. | 35 RATE OF GST TAUX DE TPS | 36 VALUE FOR CURRENCY CONVERSION CONVERSION VALEUR POUR CHANGE
37 VALUE FOR DUTY VALEUR EN DOUANE | 38 CUSTOMS DUTIES DROITS DE DOUANE | 39 SIMA ASSESSMENT COTISATION DE LMSI | 40 EXCISE TAX TAXE D'ACCISE | 41 VALUE FOR TAX VALEUR POUR TAXE | 42 GST TPS

21 LINE LIGNE | 22 DESCRIPTION DÉSIGNATION | 23 WEIGHT IN KILOGRAMS POIDS EN KILOGRAMMES | PREVIOUS TRANSACTION - TRANSACTION ANTÉRIEURE: 24 NUMBER NUMÉRO, 25 LINE LIGNE | 26 SPECIAL AUTHORITY AUTORISATION SPÉCIALE
27 CLASSIFICATION NO. N° DE CLASSEMENT | 28 TARIFF CODE TARIFAIRE | 29 QUANTITY QUANTITÉ | 30 U - M | 31 VFD CODE CODE VD | 32 SIMA CODE CODE DE LMSI | 33 RATE OF CUSTOMS DUTY TAUX DE DROIT DE DOUANE | 34 E.T. RATE TAUX T.A. | 35 RATE OF GST TAUX DE TPS | 36 VALUE FOR CURRENCY CONVERSION CONVERSION VALEUR POUR CHANGE
37 VALUE FOR DUTY VALEUR EN DOUANE | 38 CUSTOMS DUTIES DROITS DE DOUANE | 39 SIMA ASSESSMENT COTISATION DE LMSI | 40 EXCISE TAX TAXE D'ACCISE | 41 VALUE FOR TAX VALEUR POUR TAXE | 42 GST TPS

21 LINE LIGNE | 22 DESCRIPTION DÉSIGNATION | 23 WEIGHT IN KILOGRAMS POIDS EN KILOGRAMMES | PREVIOUS TRANSACTION - TRANSACTION ANTÉRIEURE: 24 NUMBER NUMÉRO, 25 LINE LIGNE | 26 SPECIAL AUTHORITY AUTORISATION SPÉCIALE
27 CLASSIFICATION NO. N° DE CLASSEMENT | 28 TARIFF CODE TARIFAIRE | 29 QUANTITY QUANTITÉ | 30 U - M | 31 VFD CODE CODE VD | 32 SIMA CODE CODE DE LMSI | 33 RATE OF CUSTOMS DUTY TAUX DE DROIT DE DOUANE | 34 E.T. RATE TAUX T.A. | 35 RATE OF GST TAUX DE TPS | 36 VALUE FOR CURRENCY CONVERSION CONVERSION VALEUR POUR CHANGE
37 VALUE FOR DUTY VALEUR EN DOUANE | 38 CUSTOMS DUTIES DROITS DE DOUANE | 39 SIMA ASSESSMENT COTISATION DE LMSI | 40 EXCISE TAX TAXE D'ACCISE | 41 VALUE FOR TAX VALEUR POUR TAXE | 42 GST TPS

21 LINE LIGNE | 22 DESCRIPTION DÉSIGNATION | 23 WEIGHT IN KILOGRAMS POIDS EN KILOGRAMMES | PREVIOUS TRANSACTION - TRANSACTION ANTÉRIEURE: 24 NUMBER NUMÉRO, 25 LINE LIGNE | 26 SPECIAL AUTHORITY AUTORISATION SPÉCIALE
27 CLASSIFICATION NO. N° DE CLASSEMENT | 28 TARIFF CODE TARIFAIRE | 29 QUANTITY QUANTITÉ | 30 U - M | 31 VFD CODE CODE VD | 32 SIMA CODE CODE DE LMSI | 33 RATE OF CUSTOMS DUTY TAUX DE DROIT DE DOUANE | 34 E.T. RATE TAUX T.A. | 35 RATE OF GST TAUX DE TPS | 36 VALUE FOR CURRENCY CONVERSION CONVERSION VALEUR POUR CHANGE
37 VALUE FOR DUTY VALEUR EN DOUANE | 38 CUSTOMS DUTIES DROITS DE DOUANE | 39 SIMA ASSESSMENT COTISATION DE LMSI | 40 EXCISE TAX TAXE D'ACCISE | 41 VALUE FOR TAX VALEUR POUR TAXE | 42 GST TPS

DECLARATION - DÉCLARATION

I / JE ______________________
PLEASE PRINT NAME - LETTRES MOULÉES S.V.P.

OF / DE ______________________
IMPORTER / AGENT - IMPORTATEUR / AGENT

DECLARE THE PARTICULARS OF THIS DOCUMENT TO BE TRUE, ACCURATE AND COMPLETE.
DÉCLARE QUE LES RENSEIGNEMENTS CI-DESSUS SONT VRAIS ET COMPLETS.

DATE ______________ SIGNATURE ______________

43 DEPOSIT - DÉPÔT

44 WAREHOUSE NO. - N° D'ENTREPÔT

45 CARGO CONTROL NO. - N° DE CONTRÔLE DU FRET

46 CARRIER CODE AT IMPORTATION / CODE DE TRANSPORTEUR À L'IMPORTATION

47 CUSTOMS DUTIES DROITS DE DOUANE
48 SIMA ASSESSMENT COTISATION DE LMSI
49 EXCISE TAX TAXE D'ACCISE
50 GST TPS
51 TOTAL

B3 (00)

Printed in Canada - Imprimé au Canada

Canada

3. Duty Payments

There are two ways in which you can make your duty payments to Revenue Canada: the cash option, or by Release on Minimum Documentation (RMD). The cash option allows several methods of payment:

♦ Cash in US or Canadian dollars

♦ Certified check

♦ Major credit card for amounts up to $500

♦ Uncertified check for amounts up to $500

♦ Uncertified check for amounts up to $2500, with appropriate personal identification

The RMD option allows you to get your goods released quickly and make your duty payments later. Most importation is done in this manner. You still have to have all of the documentation and pay the duty. To set this up with Canada Customs, you will have to post security with them in the form of cash or certified check.

4. Goods and Services Tax

As explained in chapter 18, Canada levies the Goods and Services Tax, or GST, on almost all transactions of goods and services. If you import commercial goods into Canada you will have to pay, with a few exceptions, the 7 percent GST on the value of the goods. The payment is usually made at the Canada Customs office along with other duty payments. When you resell the goods, you must charge your buyer GST as well, which will probably offset the GST you paid to Canada Customs.

If you are doing several of these transactions, you should register your activities with Revenue Canada. This will enable you to get rebates on much of the GST you pay out while doing business in Canada. You can register for rebates by making periodic reports on the GST you collected from your customers, and the GST you paid on the imports and other business activities in Canada. If you collected more GST than you paid out, submit this information in a report to Revenue Canada. But if you paid out more than you collected, Revenue Canada will send you a rebate.

5. Customs Inspection

As in most countries, Canada Customs has the authority to examine all shipments entering the country. This is usually done on a random basis, but it is somewhat linked to your import record with them. The reasons for examination are as follows:

+ To detect smuggled goods.
+ To detect prohibited or restricted items such as pornography or narcotics. (In Saudi Arabia, the Customs officials actually play video tapes as part of the inspection.)
+ For legislative requirements such as meat inspection and import permits.
+ To ensure that the goods comply with Customs legislation.

Normally there is no charge for the inspection, although you may have to pay indirectly for the time your carriers spend unloading and reloading the shipment. Also, you may have to pay a special service charge if the Canada Customs official has to travel to a location other than the Canada Customs facilities.

6. Warehousing

There are two types of warehousing associated with importing goods: sufferance warehouse, and bonded warehouse. Sufferance warehouse is used if the goods are destined for release at another facility and are awaiting reshipment, or if Canada Customs is waiting to examine them. You will usually be required to pay storage fees at this warehouse after three business days.

A bonded warehouse can be used to store goods for up to four years without paying duty on them. You pay duty only on the portion of the goods that you take out of the warehouse into the Canadian economy. While in the bonded warehouse, the goods can undergo the following alterations:

+ Labeling and marking
+ Packaging and repackaging
+ Testing
+ Diluting, cutting, slitting, trimming, and filing
+ Disassembling or reassembling goods for packing, handling, or transportation

7. Additional Information

1. *Guide to Importing Commercial Goods*, published by Revenue Canada. Available at Canada Customs offices and on the Internet at <www.ccra-adrc.gc.ca/E/pub/cp/rc4041eq/README.html>.

2. For information on the import regulations contact: Revenue Canada Customs, Customs Building, 1st Floor, 2265 St. Laurent Boulevard, Ottawa, Ontario K1G 4K3. Telephone: (613) 991-0501 Fax: (613) 991-1407.

3. *Importing Commercial Goods into Canada*, published by Revenue Canada. Available at Canada Customs offices.

Appendix A
NAFTA-QUALIFYING PROFESSIONS

This appendix provides a list of professions recognized under the North American Free Trade Agreement. It is extracted from Appendix 1603.D.1: Professionals of the agreement.

PROFESSION	MINIMUM EDUCATION REQUIREMENTS AND ALTERNATIVE CREDENTIALS
General	
Accountant	Baccalaureate or Licenciatura Degree; or CPA, CGA or CMA
Architect	Baccalaureate or Licenciatura Degree; or state/provincial license

Computer Systems Analyst	Baccalaureate or Licenciatura Degree; or Postsecondary Diploma or Postsecondary Certificate 4, and three years' experience
Disaster Relief Insurance Claims and Adjuster	Baccalaureate or Licenciatura Degree, successful completion of training in the appropriate areas of insurance adjustment
Economist	Baccalaureate or Licenciatura Degree
Engineer	Baccalaureate or Licenciatura Degree; or state/provincial license
Forester	Baccalaureate or Licenciatura Degree; or state/provincial license
Graphic Designer	Baccalaureate or Licenciatura Degree; or Postsecondary Diploma or Postsecondary Certificate, and three years' experience
Hotel Manager	Baccalaureate or Licenciatura Degree in hotel/restaurant management; or Postsecondary Diploma or Postsecondary Certificate in hotel/restaurant management, and three years' experience in hotel/restaurant management
Industrial Designer	Baccalaureate or Licenciatura Degree; or Postsecondary Diploma or Postsecondary Certificate, and three years' experience
Interior Designer	Baccalaureate or Licenciatura Degree; or Postsecondary Diploma or Postsecondary Certificate, and three years' experience
Land Surveyor	Baccalaureate or Licenciatura Degree; or state/provincial/federal license
Landscape Architect	Baccalaureate or Licenciatura Degree
Lawyer (including Notary)	LLB, JD, LLL, BCL, or Licenciatura Degree (five years); or membership in a state/provincial bar

Librarian	MLS or BLS (for which another Baccalaureate or Licenciatura Degree was a prerequisite)
Management Consultant	Baccalaureate or Licenciatura Degree; or equivalent professional experience as established by statement or professional credential attesting to five years' experience as a management consultant, or five years' experience in a field of specialty related to the consulting agreement
Mathematician (including Statistician)	Baccalaureate or Licenciatura Degree
Range Manager/Range Conservationalist	Baccalaureate or Licenciatura Degree
Research Assistant (working in a post-secondary educational institution)	Baccalaureate or Licenciatura Degree
Scientific Technician/ Technologist	Possession of (a) theoretical knowledge of any of the following disciplines: agricultural sciences, astronomy, biology, chemistry, engineering, forestry, geology, geophysics, meteorology or physics; and (b) the ability to solve practical problems in any of those disciplines, or the ability to apply principles of any of those disciplines to basic or applied research
Social Worker	Baccalaureate or Licenciatura Degree
Sylviculturist (including Forestry Specialist)	Baccalaureate or Licenciatura Degree
Technical Publications Writer	Baccalaureate or Licenciatura Degree; or Postsecondary Diploma or Post-secondary Certificate, and three years' experience

Urban Planner (including Geographer)	Baccalaureate or Licenciatura Degree
Vocational Counsellor	Baccalaureate or Licenciatura Degree

Medical/Allied Professional

Dentist	DDS, DMD, Doctor en Odontologia, or Doctor en Cirugia Dental; or state/provincial license
Dietitian	Baccalaureate or Licenciatura Degree; or state/provincial license
Medical Laboratory Technologist	Baccalaureate or Licenciatura Degree; or Postsecondary Diploma or Postsecondary Certificate, and three years' experience
Nutritionist	Baccalaureate or Licenciatura Degree
Occupational Therapist	Baccalaureate or Licenciatura Degree; or state/provincial license
Pharmacist	Baccalaureate or Licenciatura Degree; or state/provincial license
Physician (teaching or research only)	MD or Doctor en Medicina; or state/provincial license
Physiotherapist/ Physical Therapist	Baccalaureate or Licenciatura Degree; or state/provincial license
Psychologist	State/provincial license; or Licenciatura Degree
Recreational Therapist	Baccalaureate or Licenciatura Degree
Registered Nurse	State/provincial license; or Licenciatura Degree
Veterinarian	DVM, DMV, or Doctor en Veterinaria; or state/provincial license

Scientist

Agriculturist (including Agronomist)	Baccalaureate or Licenciatura Degree
Animal Breeder	Baccalaureate or Licenciatura Degree
Animal Scientist	Baccalaureate or Licenciatura Degree
Apiculturist	Baccalaureate or Licenciatura Degree
Astronomer	Baccalaureate or Licenciatura Degree
Biochemist	Baccalaureate or Licenciatura Degree
Biologist	Baccalaureate or Licenciatura Degree
Chemist	Baccalaureate or Licenciatura Degree
Dairy Scientist	Baccalaureate or Licenciatura Degree
Entomologist	Baccalaureate or Licenciatura Degree
Epidemiologist	Baccalaureate or Licenciatura Degree
Geneticist	Baccalaureate or Licenciatura Degree
Geologist	Baccalaureate or Licenciatura Degree
Geochemist	Baccalaureate or Licenciatura Degree
Geophysicist (including Oceanographer in Mexico and the United States)	Baccalaureate or Licenciatura Degree
Horticulturist	Baccalaureate or Licenciatura Degree
Meteorologist	Baccalaureate or Licenciatura Degree
Pharmacologist	Baccalaureate or Licenciatura Degree
Physicist (including Oceanographer in Canada)	Baccalaureate or Licenciatura Degree
Plant Breeder	Baccalaureate or Licenciatura Degree
Poultry Scientist	Baccalaureate or Licenciatura Degree
Soil Scientist	Baccalaureate or Licenciatura Degree
Zoologist	Baccalaureate or Licenciatura Degree

Teacher

College	Baccalaureate or Licenciatura Degree
Seminary	Baccalaureate or Licenciatura Degree
University	Baccalaureate or Licenciatura Degree

Appendix B
EXPORT ASSISTANCE CENTER LOCATIONS

This appendix provides an alphabetical by state list of Export Assistance Centers throughout the USA. It was extracted from the DoC International Trade Administration site on the Internet at <www.ita.doc.gov/fcs/uscs/domfld.html>.

ALABAMA

950 22nd Street North, Room 707
Birmingham, Alabama 35203
Telephone: (205) 731-1331; Fax: (205) 731-0076

ALASKA

550 W. 7th Avenue, Suite 1770
Anchorage, Alaska 99501
Telephone: (907) 271-6237; Fax: (907) 271-6242

ARIZONA

2901 North Central Avenue, Suite 970
Phoenix, Arizona 85012
Telephone: (602) 640-2513; Fax: (602) 640-2518

166 West Alameda
Tuscon, Arizona 85701
Telephone: (520) 670-5540; Fax: (520) 791-5413

ARKANSAS

425 W. Capitol Avenue, Suite 700
Little Rock, Arkansas 72201
Telephone: (501) 324-5794; Fax: (501) 324-7380

CALIFORNIA

390-B Fir Avenue
Fresno, California
Clovis 93611
Telephone: (209) 325-1619; Fax: (209) 325-1647

2940 Inland Empire Blvd., Suite 121
Ontario, California 91764
Telephone: (909) 466-4134; Fax: (909) 466-4140

One World Trade Center, Suite 1670
Long Beach, California 90831
Telephone: (562) 980-4550; Fax: (562) 980-4561

350 South Figueroa Street, Suite 172
Los Angeles, California 90071
Telephone: (213) 894-8784; Fax: (213) 894-8789

11150 Olympic Blvd., Suite 975
West Los Angeles, California 90064
Telephone: (310) 235-7104; Fax: (310) 235-7220

c/o Center for Trade & Commercial Diplomacy
411 Pacific Street, Suite 200
Monterey, California 93940
Telephone: (408) 641-9850; Fax: (408) 641-9849

330 Ignacio Blvd, Suite 102
Novato, California 94949
Telephone: (415) 883-1966; Fax: (415) 883-2711

530 Water Street, Suite 740
Oakland, California 94607
Telephone: (510) 273-7350; Fax: (510) 251-7352

3300 Irvine Avenue, Suite 305
Newport Beach, California 92660
Telephone: (949) 660-1688; Fax: (949) 660-8039

300 Esplanade Drive, Suite 1900
Oxnard, California 93030
Telephone: (805) 981-8150; Fax: (805) 981-8155

917 7th Street, 2nd Floor
Sacramento, California 95814
Telephone: (916) 498-5155; Fax: (916) 498-5923

5201 Great America Parkway, Suite 456
Santa Clara, California 95054
Telephone: (408) 970-4610; Fax: (408) 970-4618

6363 Greenwich Drive, Suite 230
San Diego, California 92122
Telephone: (619) 557-5395; Fax: (619) 557-6176

250 Montgomery Street, 14th Floor
San Francisco, California 94104
Telephone: (415) 705-2300; Fax: (415) 705-2297

101 Park Center Plaza, Suite 1001
San Jose, California 95113
Telephone: (408) 271-7300; Fax: (408) 271-7307

COLORADO

1625 Broadway, Suite 680
Denver, Colorado 80202
Telephone: (303) 844-6623; Fax: (303) 844-5651

CONNECTICUT

213 Court Street, Suite 903
Middletown, Connecticut 06457-3346
Telephone: (860) 638-6950; Fax: (860) 638-6970

DELAWARE

Served by the Philadelphia, Pennsylvania US Export Assistance Center

FLORIDA

1130 Cleveland Street
Clearwater, Florida 34615
Telephone: (813) 461-0011; Fax: (813) 449-2889

P.O. Box 590570
Miami, Florida 33159
5600 Northwest 36th Street, Suite 617, ZIP: 33166
Telephone: (305) 526-7425; Fax: (305) 526-7434

200 East Robinson Street, Suite 1270
Orlando, Florida 32801
Telephone: (407) 648-6235; Fax: (407) 648-6756

The Capitol, Suite 2001
Tallahassee, Florida 32399-0001
Telephone: (850) 488-6469; Fax: (850) 487-3014

GEORGIA

285 Peachtree Center Avenue Northeast, Suite 200
Atlanta, Georgia 30303-1229
Telephone: (404) 657-1900; Fax: (404) 657-1970

6001 Chatham Center Drive, Suite 100
Savannah, Georgia 31405
Telephone: (912) 652-4204; Fax: (912) 652-4241

HAWAII

P.O. Box 50026
1001 Bishop Square, Pacific Tower
Honolulu, Hawaii 96813
Telephone: (808) 541-1782; Fax: (808) 541-3435

IDAHO

700 West State Street, 2nd Floor
Boise, Idaho 83720
Telephone: (208) 334-3857; Fax: (208) 334-2783

ILLINOIS

55 West Monroe Street, Suite 2440
Chicago, Illinois 60603
Telephone: (312) 353-8045; Fax: (312) 353-8120

610 Central Avenue, Suite 150
Highland Park, Illinois 60035
Telephone: (847) 681-8010; Fax: (847) 681-8012

P.O. Box 1747, 515 North Court Street
Rockford, Illinois 61103
Telephone: (815) 987-8123; Fax: (815) 963-7943

INDIANA

11405 North Pennsylvania Street, Suite 106
Indianapolis, Indiana 46032
Telephone: (317) 582-2300; Fax: (317) 582-2301

IOWA

601 Locust Street, Suite 100
Des Moines, Iowa 50309
Telephone: (515) 288-8614; Fax: (515) 288-1437

KANSAS

151 North Volutsia
Wichita, Kansas 67214
Telephone: (316) 269-6160; Fax: (316) 683-7326

KENTUCKY

601 West Broadway, Room 634B
Louisville, Kentucky 40202
Telephone: (502) 582-5066; Fax: (502) 582-6573

2292 South Highway 27, Suite 320
Somerset, Kentucky 42501
Telephone: (606) 677-6160; Fax: (606) 677-6161

LOUISIANA

365 Canal Street, Suite 2150
New Orleans, Louisiana 70130
Telephone: (504) 589-6546; Fax: (504) 589-2337

7100 West Park Drive
Shreveport, Louisiana 71129
Telephone: (318) 676-3064; Fax: (318) 676-3063

MAINE

c/o Maine International Trade Center
511 Congress Street
Portland, Maine 04101
Telephone: (207) 541-7400; Fax: (207) 541-7420

MARYLAND

World Trade Center, Suite 2432
401 East Pratt Street
Baltimore, Maryland 21202
Telephone: (410) 962-4539; Fax: (410) 962-4529

MASSACHUSETTS

164 Northern Avenue
World Trade Center, Suite 307
Boston, Massachusetts 02210
Telephone: (617) 424-5990; Fax: (617) 424-5992

100 Granger Boulevard, Unit 102
Marlborough, Massachusetts 01752
Telephone: (508) 624-6000; Fax: (508) 624-7145

MICHIGAN

211 West Fort Street, Suite 2220
Detroit, Michigan 48226
Telephone: (313) 226-3650; Fax: (313) 226-3657

425 South Main Street, Suite 103
Ann Arbor, Michigan 48104
Telephone: (734) 741-2430; Fax: (734) 741-2432

301 West Fulton Street, Suite 718-S
Grand Rapids, Michigan 49504
Telephone: (616) 458-3564; Fax: (616) 458-3872

Oakland Pointe Office Building
250 Elizabeth Lake Road
Pontiac, Michigan 48341
Telephone: (248) 975-9600; Fax: (248) 975-9606

MINNESOTA

45 South 7th Street, Suite 2240
Minneapolis, Minnesota 55402
Telephone: (612) 348-1638; Fax: (612) 348-1650

MISSISSIPPI

704 East Main Street,
Raymond, Mississippi 39154
Telephone: (601) 857-0128; Fax: (601) 857-0026

MISSOURI

8182 Maryland Avenue, Suite 303
St. Louis, Missouri 63105
Telephone: (314) 425-3302; Fax: (314) 425-3381

2345 Grand, Suite 650
Kansas City, Missouri 64108
Telephone: (816) 410-9201; Fax: (816) 410-9208

MONTANA

c/o Montana World Trade Center
Gallagher Business Building, Suite 257
Missoula, Montana 59812
Telephone: (406) 243-2098; Fax: (406) 243-5259

NEBRASKA

11135 "O" Street
Omaha, Nebraska 68137
Telephone: (402) 221-3664; Fax: (402) 221-3668

NEVADA

1755 East Plumb Lane, Suite 152
Reno, Nevada 89502
Telephone: (702) 784-5203; Fax: (702) 784-5343

NEW HAMPSHIRE

17 New Hampshire Avenue
Portsmouth, New Hampshire 03801-2838
Telephone: (603) 334-6074; Fax: (603) 334-6110

NEW JERSEY

3131 Princeton Pike, Building 6, Suite 100
Trenton, New Jersey 08648
Telephone: (609) 989-2100; Fax: (609) 989-2395

One Gateway Center, 9th Floor
Newark, New Jersey 07102
Telephone: (973) 645-4682; Fax: (973) 645-4783

NEW MEXICO

New Mexico
c/o New Mexico Dept. of Economic Development
P.O. Box 20003, Santa Fe, New Mexico 87504-5003
1100 St. Francis Drive
Santa Fe, New Mexico 87503
Telephone: (505) 827-0350; Fax: (505) 827-0263

NEW YORK

111 West Huron Street, Room 1304
Buffalo, New York 14202
Telephone: (716) 551-4191; Fax: (716) 551-5290

163 West 125th Street, Suite 904
New York, New York 10027
Telephone: (212) 860-6200; Fax: (212) 860-6203

1550 Franklin Avenue, Room 207
Long Island, New York 11501
Telephone: (516) 739-1765; Fax: (516) 739-3310

6 World Trade Center, Room 635
New York, New York 10048
Telephone: (212) 466-5222; Fax: (212) 264-1356

707 Westchester Avenue, Suite 209
Westchester, New York 10604
Telephone: (914) 682-6712; Fax: (914) 682-6698

NORTH CAROLINA

521 East Morehead Street, Suite 435
Charlotte, North Carolina 28202
Telephone: (704) 333-4886; Fax: (704) 332-2681

400 West Market Street, Suite 102
Greensboro, North Carolina 27401
Telephone: (336) 333-5345; Fax: (336) 333-5158

NORTH DAKOTA

Served by the Minneapolis, Minnesota Export Assistance Center

OHIO

36 East 7th Street, Suite 2650
Cincinnati, Ohio 45202
Telephone: (513) 684-2944; Fax: (513) 684-3227

600 Superior Avenue East, Suite 700
Cleveland, Ohio 44114
Telephone: (216) 522-4750; Fax: (216) 522-2235

37 North High Street, 4th Floor
Columbus, Ohio 43215
Telephone: (614) 365-9510; Fax: (614) 365-9598

300 Madison Avenue
Toledo, Ohio 43604
Telephone: (419) 241-0683; Fax: (419) 241-0684

OKLAHOMA

301 Northwest 63rd Street, Suite 330
Oklahoma City, Oklahoma 73116
Telephone: (405) 231-5302; Fax: (405) 231-4211

700 North Greenwood Avenue, Suite 1400
Tulsa, Oklahoma 74106
Telephone: (918) 581-7650; Fax: (918) 594-8413

OREGON

1445 Willamette Street, Suite 13
Eugene, Oregon 97401-4003
Telephone: (541) 465-6575; Fax: (541) 465-6704

One World Trade Center, Suite 242
121 SW Salmon Street
Portland, Oregon 97204
Telephone: (503) 326-3001; Fax: (503) 326-6351

PENNSYLVANIA

One Commerce Square
228 Walnut Street, Room 850
Harrisburg, Pennsylvania 17108-1698
Telephone: (717) 221-4510; Fax: (717) 221-4505

615 Chestnut Street, Suite 1501
Philadelphia, Pennsylvania 19106
Telephone: (215) 597-6101; Fax: (215) 597-6123

2002 Federal Building, 1000 Liberty Avenue
Pittsburgh, Pennsylvania 15222
Telephone: (412) 395-5050; Fax: (412) 395-4875

PUERTO RICO

525 F.D. Roosevelt Avenue, Suite 905
San Juan, Puerto Rico (Hato Rey) 00918
Telephone: (787) 766-5555; Fax: (787) 766-5692

RHODE ISLAND

One West Exchange Street
Providence, Rhode Island 02903
Telephone: (401) 528-5104; Fax: (401) 528-5067

SOUTH CAROLINA

5300 International Boulevard, Suite 201-C
Charleston, South Carolina 29418
Telephone: (843) 760-3794; Fax: (803) 760-3798

1835 Assembly Street, Suite 172
Columbia, South Carolina 29201
Telephone: (803) 765-5345; Fax: (803) 253-3614

Park Central Office Park, Building 1, Suite 109
555 North Pleasantburg Drive
South Carolina 29607
Telephone: (864) 271-1976; Fax: (864) 271-4171

SOUTH DAKOTA

Augustana College, 2001 South Summit Avenue, Room SS-44
Siouxland, South Dakota 57197
Telephone: (605) 330-4264; Fax: (605) 330-4266

TENNESSEE

Historic City, 600 West Summit Hill Drive, Suite 300
Knoxville, Tennessee 37902-2011
Telephone: (423) 545-4637; Fax: (423) 545-4435

Buckman Hall
650 East Parkway South, Suite 348
Memphis, Tennessee 38104
Telephone: (901) 323-1543; Fax: (901) 320-9128

Parkway Towers, Suite 114
404 James Robertson Parkway
Nashville, Tennessee 37219
Telephone: (615) 736-5161; Fax: (615) 736-2454

TEXAS

1700 Congress, 2nd Floor
Austin, Texas 78701
Telephone: (512) 916-5939; Fax: (512) 916-5940

2050 North Stemmons Freeway, Suite 170
Dallas, Texas 75207
Telephone: (214) 767-0542; Fax: (214) 767-8240

711 Houston Street
Fort Worth, Texas 76102
Telephone: (817) 212-2673; Fax: (817) 978-0178

500 Dallas, Suite 1160
Houston, Texas 77002
Telephone: (713) 718-3062; Fax: (713) 718-3060

203 St. Mary's, Suite 360
c/o City of San Antonio IAD
San Antonio, Texas 78205
Telephone: (210) 228-9878; Fax: (210) 228-9874

UTAH

324 South State Street, Suite 221
Salt Lake City, Utah 84111
Telephone: (801) 524-5116; Fax: (801) 524-5886

VERMONT

National Life Building, Drawer 20
Montpelier, Vermont 05620-0501
Telephone: (802) 828-4508; Fax: (802) 828-3258

VIRGINIA

1616 North Ft. Myer Drive, Suite 1300
Arlington, Virginia 22209
Telephone: (703) 524-2885; Fax: (703) 524-2649

400 North 8th Street, Suite 540
Richmond, Virginia 23240-0026
P.O. Box 10026
Telephone: (804) 771-2246; Fax: (804) 771-2390

WASHINGTON

2001 6th Avenue, Suite 650
Seattle, Washington 98121
Telephone: (206) 553-5615; Fax: (206) 553-7253

c/o Greater Spokane Chamber of Commerce
801 West Riverside Avenue, Suite 400
Spokane, Washington 99201
Telephone: (509) 353-2625; Fax: (509) 353-2449

950 Pacific Avenue, Suite 410
Tacoma, Washington 98402
Telephone: (253) 593-6736; Fax: (253) 383-4676

WEST VIRGINIA

405 Capitol Street, Suite 807
Charleston, West Virginia 25301
Telephone: (304) 347-5123; Fax: (304) 347-5408

316 Washington Avenue
Wheeling, West Virginia 26003
Telephone (304) 243-5493; Fax: (304) 243-5494

WISCONSIN

517 East Wisconsin Avenue, Room 596
Milwaukee, Wisconsin 53202
Telephone: (414) 297-3473; Fax: (414) 297-3470

WYOMING

Served by the Denver, Colorado US Export Assistance Center

Appendix C
MARKETING TRIP CHECKLIST

This appendix provides a handy checklist to help you prepare for a marketing visit to Canada. It is divided into lead issues that should be addressed several months prior to the trip, and things that should be prepared a few days prior to leaving on the trip.

1. Several Months Prior to Trip

As soon as you know you will be making a marketing trip, consider the following:

Establish Objectives

List what you want to accomplish on the trip. This may affect your overall preparations.

Background Reading

Learn about Canada, including its economy, climate, history, and customs.

Holidays & Working Days

Ensure that you are not planning to visit during a prolonged local holiday.

Review Promotional Literature

Check over the brochures, video tapes and company give-aways you will take with you to ensure that you have a sufficient supply.

Check Business Card Supply

Ensure that you will have enough for the trip

Check Product Samples and Demonstration Equipment

Make sure you have the latest versions, and that they are functioning.

Appointments

Begin making appointments early. People you wish to see may be absent during your planned visit, and you may have to rearrange your schedule.

Travel Arrangements

Make your travel and hotel reservations early in order to take advantage of any reduced rates or fares, but more important, to ensure space availability.

2. Several Days Prior to Trip

Begin packing or setting aside items for the trip several days prior to departure. Items to consider are as follows:

Country Information

General information about the country that you will need while there, such as maps.

Promotional Literature

Rather than carry a heavy load of company brochures, you may want to send some ahead.

Portable Computer

Load your portable computer, or a travel disk with applicable files, price lists, proposals, etc.

Business Cards

Take plenty. You will be passing them out frequently.

Company Stationary

Take blank stationary with the company letterhead for writing letters, quotations and proposals to customers and agents.

Price Lists

Take up-to-date price lists, including the cost of insurance and freight to Canada.

Samples and/or Demonstration Equipment

Check the operation of samples and demonstration equipment you plan to take with you.

Hotel Reservation Confirmations

Reconfirm hotel reservations.

Traveler's Checks

Obtain traveler's checks in US or Canadian dollars.

Canadian Currency

Obtain a small amount of the Canadian currency to enable you to pay for immediate arrival expenses, such as taxis.

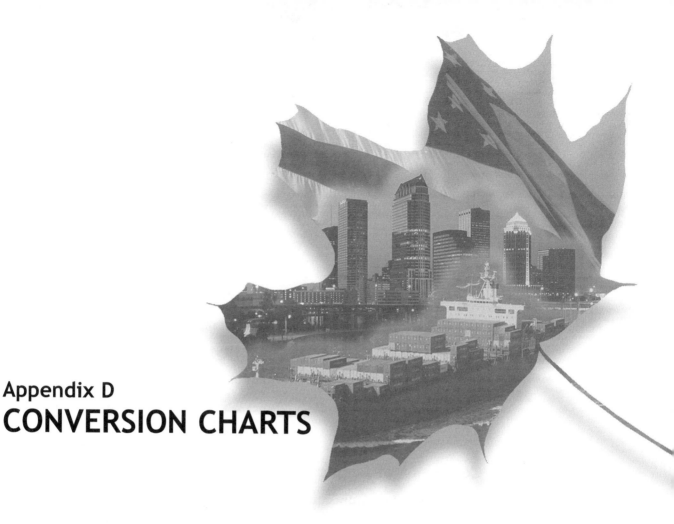

Appendix D
CONVERSION CHARTS

Conversion of Length

US Measurement	Conversion to Metric
Mile	times 1.6093 equals kilometers
Yard	times 0.9144 equals meters
Foot	times 0.3048 equals meters
Inch	times 0.0254 equals meters

Conversion of Weight

US Measurement	Conversion to Metric
Ounce	times 28.35 equals grams
Pound	times 0.45359 equals kilograms
Ton	times 0.90718 equals tonnes

Conversion of Volume

US Measurement	Conversion to Metric
Ounce (fluid US)	times 29.57 equals milliliters
Pint (liquid US)	times 0.4731 equals liters
Quart (liquid US)	times 0.9463 equals liters
Gallon	times 3.785 equals liters

Conversion of Area

US Measurement	Conversion to Metric
Square inch	times 6.451 equals cm^2
Square foot	times 0.0929 equals m^2
Square mile	times 2.5899 equals km^2
Acre	times 0.4046 equals ha

Conversion of Temperature

Fahrenheit temperature equals 1.8 times Celsius temperature plus 32

$$°F = (1.8 \times °C) + 32$$

Celsius temperature equals Fahrenheit temperature minus 32 times 5/9

$$°C = (°F - 32) \times 5/9$$